GW00694262

Literature in Perspective

General Editor: Kenneth H. Grose

Scott

Literature in Perspective

Scott

Angus and Jenni Calder

Evans Brothers Limited, London

Published by Evans Brothers Limited
Montague House, Russell Square, London, W.C.1

First published 1969

Set in 11 on 12 point Bembo and printed in Great Britain
by The Camelot Press Ltd., London and Southampton
237 35028 9 cased PR 1403
237 35029 7 limp

Literature in Perspective

Of recent years, the ordinary man who reads for pleasure has been gradually excluded from that great debate in which every intelligent reader of the classics takes part. There are two reasons for this: first, so much criticism floods from the world's presses that no one but a scholar living entirely among books can hope to read it all; and second, the critics and analysts, mostly academics, use a language that only their fellows in the same discipline can understand.

Consequently criticism, which should be as 'inevitable as breathing'—an activity for which we are all qualified—has become the private field of a few warring factions who shout their unintelligible battle cries to each other but make little communication to the common man.

Literature in Perspective aims at giving a straightforward account of literature and of writers—straightforward both in content and in language. Critical jargon is as far as possible avoided; any terms that must be used are explained simply; and the constant preoccupation of the authors of the Series is to be lucid.

It is our hope that each book will be easily understood, that it will adequately describe its subject without pretentiousness so that the intelligent reader who wants to know about Donne or Keats or Shakespeare will find enough in it to bring him up to date on critical estimates.

Even those who are well read, we believe, can benefit from a lucid exposition of what they may have taken for granted, and perhaps—dare it be said?—not fully understood.

K. H. G.

Scott

In the 20th century, Scott has been as violently scorned and neglected by sophisticated taste as he was violently admired 100 years ago. What is worse, he has lost his hold over the 'common reader'. The editions of his novels, cheap or handsome, which marched from the presses before the First World War, now choke the shelves of second-hand bookshops. Children who plod through *Ivanhoe* at the age of twelve or so bear a grudge against him for the rest of their lives. Because of their dialect speech, the novels of Scottish history in which most (though not all) of his best work is found are thought incomprehensible by English readers who find Joyce's *Ulysses* quite easy going.

And Scott has been badly served by the critics until very recently. Those who admired him tended to justify their taste in a sentimental and lazy way. Now that the tide has turned, and a fair number of new books have appeared, the danger is that Scott will become a battleground for literary theorists, an intellectual cult rather than a popular novelist. We hope that this book will help to bring Scott closer to those current generations of readers who know him little or not at all.

There is no original research in this book. But we have tried to look afresh at Scott's enormous output, and to show that his development was more consistent than has been supposed. We place his peak as a writer later than most critics—at *Quentin Durward* and *Redgauntlet* rather than at *The Heart of Midlothian*. No praise of ours is good enough for the best in Scott, but we hope that we have shown no signs of indulgence towards the worst.

Professor David Daiches has commented on several chapters

of this book. Kenneth Grose has been a most helpful (and patient) editor. But, of course, whatever mistakes may be found are entirely our own.

The best edition of Scott's novels is the 'Dryburgh' edition of 1892–4, but unfortunately we have not been able to quote from it. For the poems we have gone to Lockhart's twelve-volume edition (1833–4). Where we refer to 'Cockburn', it is to the first edition of his *Memorials of His Time* (1856). 'Lockhart' signifies the Everyman edition of his abridged *Life of Scott*.

A. and J. C.

Contents

The Authors

Jenni Calder, M.A., is the author of *Chronicles of Conscience*, a study of George Orwell and Arthur Koestler, published in 1968.
Angus Calder, B.A., D.Phil., is a Lecturer in English at University College, Nairobi, and is the author of *The People's War—1939–1945*, published in 1969.

Acknowledgements

The authors and publishers are indebted to the Scottish National Portrait Gallery for permission to reproduce the portrait of Scott on the cover, to Dr. J. S. Richardson for permission to reproduce the portrait of Viscount Dundee (on loan to the Scottish National Portrait Gallery), to the Trustees of the British Museum for permission to reproduce the engraving of Edinburgh by Joseph Turner and to Alan Daiches for the photograph of Abbotsford.

I

Scott and Scotland

When you arrive in Edinburgh, you alight at Waverley Station. The first thing to strike your eye as you leave it is likely to be the odd Gothic monument, at the end of Princes Street Gardens, which was proudly erected to the memory of Sir Walter Scott.

Standing in Princes Street itself, facing south, you soon realise that Edinburgh is not one town, but two. Below you, the pleasant gardens are planted on what was once the bed of a lake, the Nor' Loch. On their far side, towers the most powerful sight to be seen in the heart of any British city, the grey stones of Edinburgh Castle perched on a steep volcanic crag. Downwards along the skyline towards the east stream the tall buildings of the Old Town. But behind you, you will find not romance, but elegance. In a geometrical procession of squares, straight streets and crescents stand the gracious Georgian dwellings of the New Town. The heroic past and the civilised present lived side by side in Scott's imagination as they lived side by side in the Edinburgh of his own day. In his novels, he tried to bridge them, as the engineers were bridging the drained Nor' Loch in the year of his birth.

SCOTT'S EDINBURGH

But Scott was born in the Old Town—'mine own romantic town', as he called it in *Marmion*—and he always lived most happily in the past. Edinburgh, until the Act of Union with England in 1707, had been a capital city. Yet there was little to it but one great street of tall buildings lodged on the narrow spine of the Castle Hill, all the way down to the Royal Palace of Holyrood. High blocks of flats are not a modern invention.

In the High Street and the narrow closes and 'wynds' (alleys) which led off it, the artisans and middle class lived on the lowest floors, aristocrats, doctors and lawyers occupied the middle floors, and above them, at the top of the long, steep stairs, were found the sweeps, water-caddies, porters and day-labourers. The children of titled people found common pleasures with those of the poor in the courtyards and alleys. Gentry and businessmen stood in crowds outside the Parliament House in the early afternoon, jostled by beggars, water-carriers and street traders. An open sewer ran down the street; water was short, and the stench was terrible. When Scott was born in the College Wynd in 1771, his parents had two children already—but no less than six more had died in infancy, victims no doubt of the diseases which could not fail to flourish in such a city.

Scott's father was a well-to-do man, a Writer to the Signet—that is, a solicitor. Soon after Walter's birth, the family moved to a house in the handsome new George Square which had been building for a decade or so to the south of the Old Town. But throughout Scott's childhood and youth, the movement was mostly the other way—to the north, across the bridge to the New Town.

One way or another, the old life of Edinburgh was dying. The New Town had been built to kill it. The leaders of the city wanted to attract rich and aristocratic people to live there in far greater numbers. Lawyers, country gentlemen, rich merchants and lords were glad to live in the modern houses of the New Town, and the upper classes of the Old soon preferred to join them. By the time Scott died, the Old Town was becoming a mere slum.

With changes of address went changes in manners. The mateyness of the Old Town, with its rich mixture of classes, disappeared in the face of a sort of *apartheid*, when the wealthy people in the New came to have little knowledge of the poor in the Old. But in Scott's youth, some of the old friendliness—and much of the old coarseness and drunkenness—lingered on. Genteel people now tried to lose their Scots accents, but there were still many old ladies and gentlemen who talked almost the same language as the street-sweepers, and were proud of it. From them, he learned the character of the old Edinburgh of which he gives us glimpses in *Waverley*, *Guy Mannering* and *Redgauntlet*, and which is the scene of so much of *The Heart of Midlothian*.

But the new way of life was important to Scott's development, too. The New Town symbolised the new self-confidence of Scottish culture. Edinburgh was the centre of Scottish law (a different matter from English), and Scott became a lawyer like his father. It had a historic university, which he attended as a youth. Scores of well-educated young lawyers with time on their hands mixed freely with learned professors. The intellectual life of Edinburgh was an intense one. Every topic under the sun, from chemistry and geology to agriculture and metaphysics, was discussed over the claret which was the staple beverage.

Scotland, for the moment, led Europe in learning. Before Scott was born, the philosopher, David Hume, and the economist, Adam Smith, had acquired international reputations, and Adam Ferguson, whom a writer in *New Society* has recently called 'the first real sociologist', had written his great book on *Civil Society*. (Like Scott, he was fascinated by the borderline between barbarism and civilisation. His son was one of Scott's closest friends.) Here were three men who would influence the thought of the 19th and 20th centuries in many fields. There were others, now forgotten, who ranked with them at the time—moralists, literary critics, scientists, legal theorists.

In the 1790s, the Napoleonic Wars helped to make Edinburgh society still more brilliant. People from other parts of Britain could no longer travel abroad so easily, and many strangers came to admire the talents of the city's rising generation of young *literati*, of whom Scott was one. Scott disliked clever conversation, but he could not avoid the constant chatter of new ideas.

The new town of Edinburgh was born out of the remarkable economic expansion of Scotland, which was thrusting forward faster and faster in Scott's lifetime. 'Everywhere,' a modern historian writes, 'there was movement of people, old ties were broken and traditional ways of life disrupted.' Inventions like the 'spinning jenny' and the steam engine were transforming life as quickly as radio, television and atomic power have changed our own world within living memory.

MEDIEVAL SCOTLAND

Scotland in the Middle Ages had been a poor, sparsely populated country, which had lost its independence to England for a long period and had always been a pawn in the politics of other nations. From 1371, it had been ruled by the Stewart dynasty of kings, which straddled several phases of Scottish history until, only twenty-six years before Scott's birth, the young Charles Stewart raised the Highlands unsuccessfully in defence of his family's claim to the British crown. The Stewarts provided Scott with a persistent theme—Kingship. Even in novels where he does not deal with the unhappy family, it seems to lie in his thoughts when he asks himself the question, 'What makes a good king?' (Is it Richard the Lionheart, in the *Talisman* and *Ivanhoe*, a rash warrior who wins glory abroad but neglects his kingdom? Or Louis XI of France, in *Quentin Durward*, a calculating politician who rules, with great success, like a modern dictator?)

A late novel, *The Fair Maid of Perth*, deals with the period at the opening of the 15th century when the weak King Robert could not restrain his fierce or calculating nobles. It brings in two other themes of Scottish history which Scott used again and again. Perth, in the novel, has a thriving life of trade, on a small scale, but full of vigour. The townspeople, the burghers, are developing self-confidence; at the end one of them, Harry Gow, is offered a knighthood, but refuses it. The rise of the middle class was still not complete in Scott's own day, but here he shows us the predecessors of the merchants and factory owners who would come to dominate Britain in the 19th century. While the burghers gathered strength, the power of the old feudal system waned in men's hearts. As for the Highland clans—primitive tribes who would die for their chief—they were doomed, and their downfall is another of Scott's great themes. One reason for their destruction, which Scott illustrates vividly, was that they fought against each other more often than they united against their common enemies. *The Fair Maid* comes to a deeply moving end when the picked men of two clans annihilate each other, with immense but futile heroism, in front of the King.

Meanwhile, Scotland was usually allied with France against England, and a practical result of this was that bands of Scottish soldiers fought for the French kings. *Quentin Durward* shows us a young Scotsman, driven from his home as a result of a Highland feud, 'making good' in this service. It also shows us a King, Louis XI, who knew how to ally with the middle-class burghers in the interests of his own power.

When kings looked to the craftsmen and merchants of the cities to support them against the powerful feudal landowners, the Catholic Church, a great landowner, was in danger. In *The Monastery*, set in his own Border Country in the mid-16th century, Scott shows us the Church collapsing in the face of the alliance of forward-looking Scotsmen with Protestant England. In *The Abbot*, its sequel, the Catholic Mary Queen of Scots is defeated by her enemies.

THE UNION OF THE CROWNS AND THE CIVIL WARS

It was a stroke of luck, in the long run, for both countries that when Queen Elizabeth of England died, James VI of Scotland was her heir. As James I of England he united the two crowns, and the border wars which had harmed both nations died down. *The Fortunes of Nigel* shows us James in his glory—and also the influence which a Scots burgher, 'Jingling Geordie' Heriot, exerts at his court in London. James is in the great line of Scott's portraits of his typical fellow countrymen, but we see him overlooking the interests of Scotland. Scotsmen like Nigel flock down to London in search of justice or a fortune. So another of Scott's themes emerges. After 1603 Scotland merged increasingly with its old rival, England, and the period up to Scott's birth saw the death or decline of many national characteristics. Scots kings on the English throne meant the slow death of Scotland as a nation. Whether this was good or bad, loss or gain, is a question which often exercises Scott's mind.

James's tragic son, Charles I, also neglected the fatherland of the Stewarts, but in the great civil wars which his high-handedness provoked, he found Scotsmen to back his cause. The most famous was Montrose, the quintessential cavalier, who fought a brilliant campaign in the Highlands with an army of clansmen in the 1640s. But *A Legend of Montrose* lives through a character of very different meaning, Dugald Dalgetty, the thick-skinned mercenary soldier whom Scott modelled on the Scots commanders who came back from fighting for pay in Europe to pick up whatever they could lay hands on in the civil wars at home. Montrose himself calls Dalgetty 'a man of the times', for he is part of the new world which the middle classes are creating, trading his skill and courage for cash as they trade slaves for sugar. Money is destroying the feudal principles of loyalty and service to laird and King.

The period of the civil wars was a confused one in Scotland, when new developments made the chief political leaders change sides with bewildering frequency. *Woodstock* shows us the English side of the story. The young Charles II, hiding in the house of a stubborn old Royalist, already reveals the traditional Stewart weakness for women. When he regained the throne in 1660, Charles at once betrayed the Scots. Many Scotsmen had supported him because he had entered into a solemn Covenant with them which set the Presbyterian Church of Scotland over the monarchy itself and endorsed the Church's democratic organisation. *Old Mortality*, the most stark and stirring of all Scott's novels, illustrates the persecution of the poor people in the south-west who resisted King Charles's officers in the name of their Covenant. In 1679, these extremists were defeated at Bothwell Brig by the brilliant Claverhouse, later Viscount Dundee. Some of the Covenanters still held out for their principles and survived to tell younger generations of their years of outlawry. Douce Davie Deans, a central figure in *The Heart of Midlothian*, loves to brag of those days of suffering:

'How muckle better I hae thoucht mysell than them that lay saft, fed sweet, and drank deep, when I was in the moss-haggs and moors, wi' precious Donald Cameron, and worthy Mr. Blackadder, called Guess-again; and how proud I was o' being made a spectacle to men and angels, having stood on their pillory at the Canongate afore I was fifteen years old, for the cause of a National Covenant!'
Ch. 12

In 1688 came the Glorious Revolution which drove the Stewarts from the throne, and confirmed the death-warrant of absolute kingship and feudalism. Claverhouse, 'Bonnie Dundee', rallied the clans and died at Killiecrankie, in a moment of victory. But the clans, and the Tories who opposed the Revolution, were soon defeated. 'Jacobitism' was born, the creed of doomed classes. As we draw near Scott's own day, his themes begin to come together. Kingship, the clans and Scottish nationhood died together, as the middle class and the progressive sections of the aristocracy thrust them out of their way.

SCOTLAND AFTER THE ACT OF UNION

In 1707 the Act of Union robbed Scotland of its separate Parliament, though it kept its own Church and its own Law. The Union opened up the rich trade with England's American colonies to the merchants of Glasgow, which made itself the world capital of the tobacco trade. 1707 began the transformation of Scotland from an 'underdeveloped' nation to an industrial country with the best-farmed land in the world. English influence and English money assisted this transformation. Into the mouth of his greatest middle-class character, Baillie Nichol Jarvie in *Rob Roy*, Scott puts the burgher's case:

'There's naething sae gude on this side o' time but it might hae been better, and that may be said o' the Union. Nane were keener against it than the Glasgow folk, wi' their rabblings and their risings, and their mobs, as they ca' them now-a-days. But it's an ill wind blaws naebody gude—Let ilka ane roose the ford as they find it—I say, Let Glasgow flourish! whilk is judiciously and elegantly putten round the town's arms, by way of by-word.—Now, since St. Mungo catched herrings in the Clyde, what was

> ever like to gar us flourish like the sugar and tobacco trade? Will ony body tell me that, and grumble at the treaty that opened us a road west-awa' yonder?'

But Andrew Fairservice's retort reflects the dismay which many Scotsmen (including, of course, Scott himself) felt at the loss of nationhood. He rejoins

> 'That it was an unco change to hae Scotland's laws made in England; and that, for his share, he wadna' for a' the herring-barrels in Glasgow, and a' the tobacco casks to boot, hae gien up the riding o' the Scots Parliament, or sent awa' our crown, and our sword, and our sceptre, and Mons Meg, to be keepit by thae English pock-puddings in the Tower o' Lunnon. What wad Sir William Wallace, or auld Davie Lindsay, hae said to the Union, or them that made it?' Ch. 27

Scott's head was with the Baillie, but his heart was with Andrew Fairservice. In the novel, our sympathies go equally to Jarvie, to Rob Roy and his outlawed clan, and to the romantic Jacobite heroine, Di Vernon, who takes part in the Rising of 1715, another hapless attempt to restore the Stewarts.

Other novels set in this period show the old feudal life on the way out. (So does Scott's bad melodrama, *The Doom of Devoirgoil.*) In *The Bride of Lammermoor*, Scott gives a tragic picture of the feudal landlord, Ravenswood, driven out of his hereditary lands by the 'new man', the middle-class Ashton. The 18th century was to be an age of agricultural 'improvement', carried out by landlords who farmed for a cash profit, not just to live off their own produce. 'Improvement' meant more efficient farming, with modern implements and methods. It also meant the driving out of many small tenants, who might now have to work for wages rather than supporting themselves.

In *The Pirate*, Scott presents a farcical picture of a would-be 'improver', Triptolemus Yellowley, trying to destroy the old ways of the Shetland Islands. But Scott could not seriously favour the old farming, with its wasteful system of strips, and its crude ploughs, though it gave every man a stake in the land. In the end, the Yellowleys were bound to win, and he knew it.

Meanwhile, England and Scotland were still not in harmony. While old-fashioned families in England supported the Stewarts, more or less apathetically, it was the continued existence of the clans which gave a social basis to Jacobitism in Britain. Smuggling was an issue between the two countries; the rugged Scottish coastline was hard to police, and some of the methods of the Glasgow merchants struck their English competitors as highly unfair. The Porteous Riots of 1736 reflected 'the national addiction to smuggling'. In reprisal for these riots, the English Parliament fined the city of Edinburgh £2,000—an act which seems impudent now, and which outraged Scottish feelings then. The riots give Scott the opening for *The Heart of Midlothian.* Justice has to be found in England now, so Jeanie Deans walks to London to save her sister's life. But in his attractive portrait of the Duke of Argyle, Scotland's chief representative at Westminster, Scott shows us the positive aspects of the Union.

In 1745 some of the clans rose again in support of the Stewarts. 'Bonnie Prince Charlie' was foredoomed to failure, and Scott shows us why in *Waverley*. The primitive clan society could win brief, brilliant victories, but it could not sustain a long war. The ambitious, cultured Fergus McIvor who is Scott's typical clan leader, is a modern politician who is barely worthy of the traditional loyalty which his clan gives him. The clans were breaking down within themselves before the bloody defeat at Culloden destroyed them with impressive, but perhaps heart-rending, finality. After the '45 the chieftains were quite ready to betray the loyalty of their followers and turn their lands into huge sheep runs for their own profit, while poor Highlanders had to seek a new life in America.

SCOTT'S VIEWPOINT

In 1745 the modern history of Britain begins in earnest. The last stronghold of feudalism in the hills and islands of Scotland was invaded by the hired soldiers of a modern state. Scott belonged to only the second generation of Scotsmen to be born in a society from which the primitive tribal and feudal ways had been banished.

Scott was torn between the old ways of life which had perished and the new ways which were bringing unthought-of prosperity to the middle classes. Just as people now look back with nostalgia from our new and neurotic affluence to the apparent calm and order of Edwardian society, so Scott stared across the borderline which 1745 had drawn across history, and across the lives of the old men and women he had talked to as a young man. At the end of *Waverley*, he wrote:

> There is no European nation, which, within the course of half a century, or little more, has undergone so complete a change as this kingdom of Scotland. The effects of the insurrection of 1745,—the destruction of the patriarchal power of the Highland chiefs,—the abolition of the heritable (i.e., feudal) jurisdictions of the Lowland nobility and barons,—the total eradication of the Jacobite Party, which, averse to intermingle with the English, or adopt their customs, long continued to pride themselves upon maintaining ancient Scottish manners and customs,—commenced this innovation. The gradual influx of wealth, and extension of commerce, have since united to render the present people of Scotland a class of beings as different from their grandfathers, as the existing English are from those of Queen Elizabeth's time. Ch. 72

It is upon his understanding of the causes of this change, and of the radically different characters of the old order and the new order, that Scott's greatness as a historical novelist rests. His whole sequence of novels is built round the historical themes which he outlines here.

THE INDUSTRIAL REVOLUTION

When Scott died, there were roughly seven people living in Scotland for every four alive when he was born, though in 1830 there were still only 2,350,000 Scotsmen. Edinburgh grew fast in this new wave of prosperity—to 67,000 people by 1801—but Glasgow grew faster and overtook it, nearly doubling its population between 1780 and 1801. Edinburgh was not a backwater; it still led Scotland in law and culture. But the new Scotland was not seen there so much as in the thriving ports and mills of Clydeside, and in small but growing 'boom-towns' like Kilmarnock.

This rise in population reflected a rise in the standard of living, brought about by agricultural 'improvement', and the higher wages and cheaper goods which arrived with the Industrial Revolution.

In fact, several 'revolutions' were happening at the same time. There was a revolution in transport and communications which underlay the new prosperity, making trade easier and industrial production cheaper. In 1760 there were only two 'slow and infrequent' stage coach services in the whole of Scotland. When Scott died there were over a hundred much faster daily services. In the introduction to *The Heart of Midlothian*, Scott imagines, in the words of the fictitious Peter Pattieson, what this might mean to a typical Scottish village:

> '. . . Mail-coach races against mail-coach, and high-flyer against high-flyer, through the most remote districts in Britain. And in our village alone, three post-coaches, and four coaches with men armed, and in scarlet cassocks, thunder through the streets each day.'
> Ch. 1

All over Scotland roads were being made or improved, so that they were good enough to serve the tourists who came up in flocks to look at the Highland scenery which Scott had described in his novels and poems. When Scott was born, both the bridge over the Tay at Perth and the Forth and Clyde Canal were being built—part of a great outburst of civil engineering which transformed sleepy ports and brought coal quickly to the mills and cities.

In 1759 the first modern Scottish ironworks was opened at Carron, near Falkirk, and it prospered, producing light cannon for the Napoleonic Wars. During the first thirty years of Scott's life the production of linen in Scotland doubled, largely thanks to technical improvements. The woollen goods trade also throve, but the most formidable leap forward was in cotton. 'Everywhere, from Annan to Sutherland, people were infected with enthusiasm for this new industry.' Along with cotton came the first modern factories. When Scott was a boy of seven, the first cotton mill in Scotland was opened. By 1812 there were 120 mills, mostly centring on Glasgow. Children of four were sometimes found working the new machines. The great mills at New Lanark were soon employing well over 1,000 people, herding together in large buildings the like of which had never been seen before. In place of the independent peasant, the cottage weaver, the village craftsman of the Old Scotland, the New Scotland was throwing up the city worker, the rootless slave of the machine.

Scott certainly understood the importance of these revolutions. He praised James Watt, in *The Monastery*, as

> The man whose genius discovered the means of multiplying our national resources to a degree perhaps even beyond his own stupendous powers of calculation and combination; bringing the treasures of the abyss to the summit of the earth—giving the feeble arm of man the momentum of an Afrite—commanding manufactures to arise, as the rod of the prophet produced water in the desert, affording the means of dispensing with that time and tide which wait for no man, and of sailing without that wind which defied the commands and threats of Xerxes himself.
>
> ANSWER TO THE INTRODUCTORY EPISTLE

In such flowery and excited language, he hailed the application of steam power to industry and the arrival of the steam-boat. This was the heroic age of the Scots engineers, as well as a period of rebirth in Scottish culture.

But Scott never described the New Scotland in his fiction; it was off his beat. While the New Town of Edinburgh owed its existence to the prosperity which industrial change had brought, Edinburgh remained a city of 'consumers' rather than 'producers'; its people were mainly tradesmen, servants, lawyers, retired merchants, rather than factory workers. Scott could not miss the coal-mines round Dalkeith when he rode to his beloved Borders. Galashiels, a short walk from the dream-house which he built for himself at Abbotsford, was such a booming centre of the woollen industry that one of his contemporaries called it 'the Glasgow of Selkirkshire'. But if Scott had been born the son of a Glasgow industrialist instead of an Edinburgh lawyer, he would have written very different novels.

As it was, the character of the working class of the New Scotland filled him with hatred and distrust. He fell into a stupid panic in 1819 when hardship in the new industries prompted fears of revolution. Like the other stalwart citizens of Edinburgh, he saw the miners, weavers and mill-hands as a mob of blackguards. He feared that the workers of Galashiels would join forces with their fellows in north-east England and Clydeside, and no doubt expected that Abbotsford would be sacked and he would die fighting for his property. And, indeed, it was an age of revolutions.

THE FRENCH REVOLUTION

When Scott was five, Britain's American colonies had revolted. In 1789 the French Revolution marked the beginning of more than a quarter of a century of wars and tumult in Europe. Scott's brilliant younger contemporary, Henry Cockburn, describes the fear and outrage which the Revolution caused among the Edinburgh middle class: 'Grown-up people talked at this time of nothing but the French Revolution, and its supposed consequences. . . . If the ladies and gentlemen, who formed the society of my father's house, believed all that they said about the horrors of French bloodshed, and of the anxiety of people here to imitate them, they must have been wretched indeed. Their talk sent me to bed shuddering.' Not till 1815 were Napoleon and France finally vanquished, and Cockburn points out that 'Old men, but especially those in whose memories the American War ran into the French one, had only a dim recollection of what peace was; and middle-aged men knew it now for the first time'.

No writer of the time could avoid the terrifying, exhilarating feeling that history was on the move. The 'Romantic' movement which developed in the late 18th century consisted of poets, critics and novelists who all reacted, in their different ways, to the sweeping away of the old and the coming in of the new. Blake attacked the new industrialism. Wordsworth idealised the simple ways of the countryside, which new roads, enclosures, 'improvements' and, soon, steam engines, were set fair to change out of all recognition. Byron and Shelley became notorious as apostles of freedom at a time when a corrupt Tory oligarchy, in power both in England and Scotland, made the fear of revolution an excuse for suppressing with bad law and naked force any sign of discontent at home. It was left to Scott to express in his writings the new sense of history which came with those momentous years.

A NEW SENSE OF HISTORY

Of course, an interest in the past was nothing new. Shakespeare went to the classical world and the Middle Ages for the plots of his plays. Christopher Wren would occasionally turn his hand to a mock-Gothic church. In the 18th century a new degree of scholarship had been applied to history. The poet Gray had imitated ancient Norse poetry, and cultivated persons had developed a taste for medieval architecture and 'Gothic' novels. Yet the understanding of historical change had still been absent; men still ignored the social and economic basis of historical events, and failed to see that a 'Gothic' style of architecture had been part of a way of life radically different from that of their own times. But now, with Europe in turmoil, the past became a matter for more vivid and intelligent interest.

This was partly because so much change created a nostalgia for the old life which was being brutally pushed aside. Already, the dead clans and their tartans were a subject of sentimental pride. The preservation of old buildings became a matter of serious concern. Scott's young fellow-lawyers protested when the old Parliament House in Edinburgh was given a new face, and some even regretted it when the foul Tolbooth Prison, 'the Heart of Midlothian', was pulled down. The interest in old Scottish ballads and songs, which had started early in the 18th century, intensified as it neared its close.

But if sentimentality was one foundation for the new interest in history, the urge to understand change was still stronger. When King Louis of France was executed, men remembered the English Revolution 150 years before, when the Roundheads had cut off King Charles's head. The violent events of the present helped men to understand the violent changes of the past; and at the same time, it seemed that a true knowledge of the past might help them to understand the present. History no longer appeared to be a simple chronicle of kings and queens; the French Revolution laid bare the clash of the classes, the goad of economic necessity. Instead of the notion that human nature had always been much the same, men who saw human nature throwing up new ideals, new potentialities, new types of villainy and heroism, accepted the idea of constant change and development.

For many, as for Scott, the losses seemed to balance the gains. The 'Gothic' churches which were built in such great numbers in the 19th century (and which Scott's influence had a great deal to do with), still stand in our High Streets and suburbs as signs that the wealthy Victorian middle class looked back with guilt and nostalgia to a time when money had been unimportant and builders had laboured out of piety, with a pride in their beautiful crafts.

SCOTT'S FAMILY

Scott's ancestry showed how history had rung its changes in Scottish society over three or four hundred years, and Scott was very proud of it—proud of the peaceable Quakers as well as the bold Border barons. Though he was not of noble birth, he was 'well connected'. On his father's side he could trace a dramatic descent from the great families of Border Scotts. One of these violent heroes of the wars between family and family, Scots and English, had also been 'Walter Scott'—'Auld Watt of Harden'—and Scott loved to retail the anecdotes which clustered round him. Another Walter was 'Beardie', Scott's great-grandfather, who refused to trim or shave his beard as a token of his sympathy for the banished Stewart kings. But Beardie's son, Scott's grandfather, was a Whig who supported the Hanoverians, a successful farmer who did well out of the important cattle trade with England which developed after the Act of Union.

Scott's own father was middle-aged when Walter was born.

He was an austere man with deep principles, both professional and religious. He was a strict Calvinist, and the best and worst of John Knox's grim religion lay around the growing Walter. Sundays, as in so many other Scottish households of rich and poor, were gloomy days of religious devotion. Scott himself, quite typically, chose in later life to worship as an Episcopalian, in the Scottish Church which was doctrinally similar to the Church of England; he saw this as a compromise between the Protestantism which he still accepted and the Catholicism of his beloved Middle Ages.

Scott's mother was brighter and more sympathetic than his father. Her own father was Professor of Medicine at Edinburgh University—he, too, was descended from a great Border family, the Rutherfords. Besides Walter, four brothers and a sister survived. None was very important in Scott's own life; all died young and all were more or less unsuccessful. Two were soldiers, one was a sailor. The youngest brother, Daniel, is the subject of a revealing story. A drunken, incompetent person, he showed cowardice during a riot in the West Indies, where he had a post on an estate. He was sacked, and when he came home, broken, to die in 1806, Scott refused to see him or attend his funeral. Cowardice was for him the most unforgivable of weaknesses.

SCOTT'S CHILDHOOD

When Walter was eighteen months old, he fell ill. He lost the use of his right leg, and though he was to become a tall, very strong man, he dragged it behind him till his death. His grandfather Rutherford advised that he should be sent to the country for his health, so he went to the farm of his other grandfather at Sandy Knowe, in Berwickshire. His first memories, then, were of the Border country, of shepherds and sheep, of news of the American Revolution; and of a distant relation who had seen the execution of the Jacobite rebels at Carlisle in 1745, and whose stories made the boy sure that he would always be a Jacobite in his sympathies. (In 1814 he made these executions form a moving climax to *Waverley*.)

Until Walter was eight, he spent most of his time at Sandy

Knowe, listening with delight to his grandmother's stories of Watt of Harden and other Border rogues. As he wrote in *Marmion*:

> And ever, by the winter hearth,
> Old tales I heard of woe or mirth,
> Of lovers' slights, of ladies' charms,
> Of witches' spells, of warriors' arms;
> Of patriot battles, won of old
> By Wallace wight and Bruce the bold;
> Of later fields of feud and fight,
> When, pouring from their Highland height,
> The Scottish clans, in headlong sway,
> Had swept the scarlet ranks away.
>
> INTRODUCTION TO CANTO 3

It was in boyhood and youth that Scott developed his extraordinary ability to visualise and describe with clarity a complex and confused field of war, pushing pebbles and shells around on the floor to represent the opposing armies in some historic battle. When he was sent to bathe in the sea for a while at Prestonpans, scene of a major battle of the '45, he met a retired army captain called Dalgetty, who told him his tales of the German wars of the mid-18th century.

When he went home for good, his mother encouraged his taste for reading. He was sent to the Edinburgh High School, and because his lameness made him less active than his fellows he deliberately cultivated his gift for telling stories, with which he entertained them in the winter play-hours. He read anything and everything—poetry, travels, fairy-tales, romances, Shakespeare (of whose works he came to have an immense knowledge), Spenser (whose tales of knights and ladies he adored)—and later, Bishop Percy's recent collection of old ballads and poems, and the novels of Richardson, Fielding and Smollett. He always admitted to having a remarkable memory, but he was otherwise very modest about his intellectual gifts. He later wrote of his schooldays, 'few ever read so much, and to so little purpose'. In fact, he was cramming his mind with the sort of off-beat anecdotes and significant details out of which he made his novels. But he was bad at Greek, and not very good at Latin, and since they were the basis of education in those days, he was not outstanding at school.

At home, his father set him under an earnest young tutor, a fanatical Calvinist, with whom Scott got on well. He was always ready to argue with his pupil—so they thrashed their way through the history of the Church of Scotland. 'I, with a head on fire for chivalry (Scott wrote), was a Cavalier; my friend was a Roundhead: I was a Tory, and he was a Whig. I hated Presbyterians, and admired Montrose with his victorious Highlanders; he liked the Presbyterian Ulysses, the dark and politic Argyle: so that we never wanted subjects of dispute; but our disputes were always amicable.'

In later life, Scott continued to idolise the wicked, gallant, astonishingly handsome Marquis of Claverhouse, the worst enemy of the Covenanters. He had a portrait of 'Clavers' in his study when he wrote. Yet in *Old Mortality* he showed Claverhouse to be the cruel soldier he was, and made his hero a supporter of the humble Covenanters. Much of Scott's astonishing *fairness* in his novels must have come from those early debates with his tutor, which were 'always amicable'.

Between school and College (to which middle-class boys went on at the age of 12), Scott spent a few months with a kind aunt at Kelso, on the Tweed, where he went to the village school and sat beside a shopkeeper's son called James Ballantyne, whose fortunes were eventually to be closely linked with his. At fifteen, Scott was indentured to his own father, to learn the craft of law. While still only a boy, he paid his first visit to the Highlands on his father's business. Next year his health broke down, and he spent a long illness reading romances and poetry, and also beginning the serious study of history. When he recovered, he began to take long rides and walks into the country, 'for the pleasure of seeing romantic scenery'.

THE LAW

At eighteen, he decided not to follow his father as a solicitor, but to read for the Bar instead, to become an advocate. He studied both Civil and Scots Law at the University, alongside his great friend William Clerk. Scott loved Scots Law, and no one can read his novels without knowing it. He writes of it, in an autobiography of his childhood and youth which is found at the beginning of the classic life of him by his son-in-law, Lockhart, as an 'ancient castle, partly entire, partly ruinous, partly dilapidated, patched and altered during the succession of ages by a thousand additions and combinations, yet still exhibiting, with the marks of its antiquity, symptoms of the skill and wisdom of its founders . . .'

To study law, as this metaphor suggests, was to study an ancient yet living thing. From this study, Scott learned about the customs of feudal society, as they affected rich and poor; he could see how the law changed as feudalism decayed, how new trade and industries brought new laws. Always, he was closely in touch with the economic basis of human history, with getting and spending, renting and letting, buying and selling. The study of sociology, as we know it, grew naturally out of the study of law, because the law, at any given time, in any society, embodies the relationships between men and classes.

Furthermore, as Scott's most attractive legal character, Counsellor Pleydell, remarks in *Guy Mannering*,

> 'I have now satisfied myself, that if our profession sees more of human folly and human roguery than others, it is because we witness them acting in that channel in which they can most freely vent themselves. In civilised society, law is the chimney through which all that smoke discharges itself that used to circulate through the whole house, and put every one's eyes out . . .' Ch. 9

A lawyer got to know many clients, and it was his business to learn a lot about them. He saw the tragic and the comic sides of human nature in the courts. He listened to the talk of murderers, thieves, smugglers, debtors, and witnesses of all sorts. Scots Law is very important in two of Scott's finest novels—*The Heart of Midlothian* and *Redgauntlet*. But the work which it did for Scott's imagination is seen in all his writing. Wherever he describes a rogue, he understands the man, and his attitudes to life, and his code of honour; and he can find sympathy for the worst of his ruffians.

While he was engaged in this study, Scott fell in love. It was a hopelessly romantic affair. The girl (still in her mid-teens) was Williamina Stuart-Belsches, and her rank in society was well above Scott's. For several years, until she married a rich banker in 1796, Scott doted on her. What scars the affair left on him are not quite clear; but in *The Bride of Lammermoor* there is a violently bitter portrait of a scheming mother betraying her daughter's love, and perhaps Scott put some of his own feelings into the gloomy reflections of Nicholas Tressilian in *Kenilworth*. But, with a note of compromise and reconciliation which might have come from one of his own novels, Scott found Williamina's husband one of his staunchest and most useful friends after he was ruined in 1825.

YOUTH AND MARRIAGE

Meanwhile, Scott 'took the gown'. What his life as a young lawyer was like can be glimpsed in *Redgauntlet*, where Sanders Fairford is Scott's own father, Alan Fairford, the sober hero, is Scott's version of himself, and Darsie Latimer, the romantic hero, is modelled on his friend Clerk. Soon afterwards, Scott paid his first visit to the remote valley of Liddesdale, down by the Cumberland Border. Here he met one of the originals of Dandie Dinmont, in *Guy Mannering*, an honest farmer who came out to greet the young advocate surrounded by dogs, and made him very welcome when he saw how Scott got on with them.

This was in 1792. For seven successive years thereafter, Scott, with a friend who was Sheriff-substitute of Roxburghshire, visited Liddesdale, exploring every river to its source and lingering over every ruin. There was no inn in the whole valley, so they put up with the farmers and preachers, and here Scott began to collect the material for his *Minstrelsy of the Scottish Border*. His companion recalled those days for Lockhart:

> '"Eh me!", says Shortreed, "sic an endless fund o' humour and drollery as he then had wi' him! Never ten yards but we were either laughing or roaring or singing. Wherever we stopped, how

> brawlie he suited himsel' to everybody. He aye did as the lave did; never made himsel' the great man, or took ony airs in the company."'
>
> LOCKHART, p. 58

Scott, like his own heroes, had the knack of making himself liked by rich and poor wherever he went. He convulsed the other young advocates who hung round the courts of Edinburgh with his accurate imitations of the eccentric judges of the time. He loved to talk broad Scots, like his friend the Sheriff, and to tell a funny story, crying with laughter as he did so. His endless, unself-conscious flow of humour made him popular even with the brilliant minority of Whigs among the young lawyers.

The life of a young advocate in the heyday of Edinburgh was a pleasant one, full of eating, drinking and wit. Scott spoke in one of the debating clubs, and he travelled constantly to the Highlands and the Border Country for business and pleasure. In a churchyard in Angus he came across the original 'Old Mortality'—a bizarre fanatic who wandered about restoring the inscriptions on the tombstones of the Covenanters. But he also spent hours with the old documents in the Advocate's library, of which he became a curator at the age of twenty-four.

It was about this time that he began to write seriously. Germany was then in the vanguard of literary taste, and German Romanticism was the latest fashion. Scott, with several friends, had formed a class to learn German. Now, struck with the imitation of an ancient ballad in Matthew Lewis's Gothic novel of horror, *The Monk*, he dashed off a translation of a German romantic poem, Bürger's 'Lenore'. After the upset of Williamina's marriage, he spurred on with his efforts, encouraged by his friends. When his first translations were published anonymously in 1796, they were well received.

In 1797, during a tour of the English Lake District, he met Charlotte Charpentier, the gay, pretty daughter of a French royalist family in exile. After a whirlwind courtship, he married her in December. It seems that Julia Mannering is partly a portrait of her, which no doubt explains why she is one of the few heroines in Scott to have much reality. They set up house in

North Castle Street in the New Town; modern comfort with a good view of the castle on its crag.

Napoleon was rising to power in France, and in 1797 an invasion scare prompted the citizens of Edinburgh to form a Corps of Volunteer Cavalry. Scott became its Quartermaster, and drilled daily at five in the morning. Besides this, there were regular periods 'in camp'. To the outsider, even then, these amateur soldiers would have seemed rather amusing. But Scott took it in deadly earnest. Cockburn writes, 'It was not a duty with him, or a necessity, or a pastime, but an absolute passion, indulgence in which gratified his feudal taste for war, and his jovial sociableness'. Cockburn tells a story which reveals Scott's alarming pugnacity. '. . . His troop used to practise, individually, with the sabre at a turnip, which was stuck on the top of a staff, to represent a Frenchman. . . . Every other trooper, when he set forward in his turn, was far less concerned about the success of his aim at the turnip, than about how he was to tumble. But Walter pricked forward gallantly, saying to himself, "cut them down, the villains, cut them down!" and made his blow, which from his lameness was often an awkward one, cordially, muttering curses all the while at the detested enemy.'

For many years, Scott drilled with the Volunteers religiously, and he wrote the scenes of action in *Marmion* largely when he was at camp with them.

Scotland at this time was virtually under the dictatorship of Henry Melville, Lord Dundas, and his Tory clique. As Lord Advocate, Dundas had the patronage of all the official jobs in Scotland. Under 4,000 people in Scotland, all well-to-do, had the vote in Parliamentary elections, and bribery was taken for granted. Most of the lawyers were Tories, and it was in their interest to be so. Scott's Toryism was constant and sincere; but it is a fact that in 1799 influential friends secured for him from Dundas the job of Sheriff-Deputy of Selkirkshire. As a judge for this quiet, sparsely populated county, he earned a decent salary for doing very little, meanwhile continuing his practice at the bar. It was clear, however, that Scott was better at telling stories outside the courts than pleading a case inside them.

In 1802 he began to publish his *Minstrelsy of the Scottish Border*, the book which at once gave him an international reputation. The *Minstrelsy* ran through five editions by 1812, and was soon translated into German, Danish and Swedish. Such excitement about new editions of old songs would, of course, be unthinkable today; but there was then a booming interest in the past and in 'ancient' poetry. The public was delighted, not only with Scott's scholarship and style, but also with the fine printing—the work of Scott's old schoolfriend from Kelso, James Ballantyne.

The *Minstrelsy* contained, surreptitiously and openly, a good deal of Scott's own work. He now commenced a long poem about his own Border ancestors, *The Lay of the Last Minstrel*. When William Wordsworth—still an *avant garde* writer who was not widely popular—visited Scotland in 1803, he was delighted with the poem, and with Scott's company.

THE WIZARD OF THE NORTH

In 1804 an uncle died, who left Scott a good deal of money. He rented a cottage at Asshestiel, on the Tweed. In the country, he settled down to a way of life which was to last for many years. He began writing at six in the morning, and, except in bad weather, made a point of stopping by one o'clock. Then, with whatever friends were to hand, he roamed the countryside on foot or on horseback, hunting hares, visiting ruins, admiring wild scenery, or fishing. He often 'burnt the water'—spearing salmon by torchlight—a sport which he describes marvellously in *Guy Mannering*. He combined the life of the country gentleman with that of the prolific writer.

In 1805 the great spate of imaginative writing which was to earn him the nickname of 'the Wizard of the North', opened with the publication of the *Lay*. Within a few years it sold 30,000 copies. The leading statesmen of the day, Pitt and Fox, were among those who praised it—a fact which Scott, not too modestly, makes much of in the opening lines of his next long poem. The poems of Blake, of Wordsworth, of Coleridge, which had marked the beginnings of 'Romantic' verse in Britain, were far greater than the *Lay*, as time was to show. But the stirring descriptions, the rushing metre and the sheer energy of the *Lay* made it the first 'Romantic' poem to gain a wide public.

In the first flush of success, Scott went into business with his friend Ballantyne, whom he had now brought to Edinburgh. This would finally bring about his downfall—but it also paved the way to the novels, which he wrote at a great rate to keep his business afloat. He kept his financial interest in Ballantyne's printing press secret—gentlemen, on the whole, did not go into 'trade'.

In 1806 patronage brought him another job—though this was the year of Dundas's downfall, and it was the Whigs who, during a very brief interlude of rule, confirmed Scott's appointment as a Clerk of Session. It marked the end of his undistinguished career as an advocate, which he was not sorry to give up. The Clerk sat in the main court at Edinburgh all the time while it was sitting. He attended to the cases, and when the judges gave their verdicts (still, very often, in thick Scots speech), it was the Clerk's job to write them down in the correct legal language. The court sat for three months in the summer, May to July, and also from November to March, for 4 to 6 hours a day. There was heavy paper-work in the evenings at Castle Street, and a good deal of mere drudgery. But Scott could ponder 'old, unhappy, far-off things' while the lawyers droned on, and he had more than six months of the year which he could spend in the country.

In the same year, the publisher Archibald Constable paid him 1,000 guineas for a poem which he had barely started, *Marmion*. Constable was transforming British publishing at the same time as Scott was transforming its products. In 1802 Constable had begun to bring out the famous *Edinburgh Review*, which was a mouthpiece for the brilliant young Whigs—Francis Jeffrey, Cockburn and Sydney Smith among them. Never before had magazine criticism been so brilliant, so fierce and so influential. Scott was a frequent contributor until he fell out with the *Review* over its politics in 1808. But his association with Constable went on much longer. The fortunes of Constable and

Ballantyne became inextricably twisted together, and in the end Scott and his publisher were ruined at the same time.

Constable paid unheard-of prices for poems, for philosophy and, later, for novels. He attracted the best talents in Britain and raised the rewards and the status of writing. His gamble with *Marmion* paid off handsomely. In 1810 Constable gave his prize author £2,000 for *The Lady of the Lake*, and this too was immensely successful. Meanwhile, Scott was bending his talents to the large task of editing Dryden and Swift. In his study at Asshestiel, his four young children and his dogs frisked round him as he wrote. He still treated his writing as a hobby, not a mission. When his young daughter Sophia was asked what she thought of *The Lady of the Lake*, she said seriously, 'Oh, I have not read it: papa says there's nothing so bad for young people as reading bad poetry.'

ABBOTSFORD

In 1811 Scott's lease at Asshestiel was running out. He bought some land near the ancient abbey of Melrose, which gave him what he called 'a mile of the beautiful turn of Tweed above Gala foot'. He started to build what was little more than a cottage, on the site which he had named 'Abbotsford'. But the idea of constructing a baronial mansion and of being the laird of many acres of his favourite Border Country grew in his mind. Abbotsford, as he built it up over the next fourteen years, is not a really large house. But it was costly, roomy and luxurious, combining the latest modern conveniences with a great deal of expensive hand-made Gothic decoration. It was more than he could afford, best-seller though he was.

The house tells us a lot about Scott (see illustrations). The landscape around is empty, but gentle in its curving hills and its rolling river. Scott's contemporaries, when they read his poems and novels, saw in their mind's eye the wild Border of the Middle Ages, and the craggy Highlands and Islands—we can see what they imagined in the romantic and exaggerated illustrations by contemporary artists. But the Border, in Scott's own day, was a peaceable part of the world, within easy reach of the amenities of Edinburgh. This, not the lochs and mountains, was Scott's chosen environment.

Its proportions remind us that Abbotsford was built in the elegant Regency period, when Nash was putting up the cool, pretty town houses round London's Regent's Park. But the decorations are medieval, lovingly copied from originals in churches and castles. The rooms in which Scott read and wrote are filled with his amazing collection of relics, from the favourite portrait of 'Clavers' (see illustrations) and a piece of oatcake found in the pocket of a dead soldier at Culloden, to the fearsome weapons carried by Rob Roy and complete suits of medieval armour. Scott knew the details of arms and armour which he described in his novels quite literally as well as his own furniture. Then there is the big library of books, many of them rare and obscure.

Scott, as we see him at Abbotsford, was a man who lived by compromise. 'He reverences Melrose,' wrote John Ruskin, 'yet casts one of its piscinas, puts a modern steel grate on it, and makes it his fireplace.' (*Modern Painters*, Part IV, Chapter XVI, section 33.) He did not try to live as his heroes had lived, in draughty, bare castles or stinking manor houses; everything suited his comfort as a well-bred man of his day. He loved crude, savage ballads and rousing Jacobite songs, yet his own idea of a real poet was that very unromantic writer John Dryden. The gentleman in Scott wrote the happy endings to his novels, where his heroes come into a fortune and settle down to respectability. But the schoolboy in Scott cut fiercely at imaginary Frenchmen on sticks, loved knives and old guns and armour around him, and wrote affectionate accounts of rustlers, smugglers, rebels, gypsies, illiterate farmers, thieves, pirates, bare-legged Highlanders, Border ruffians, hedge-priests, outlaws, defiant hill-preachers—who involve the reasonable young heroes in their wrong-doing, their revolts, their crude pleasures. It was this boyish and nostalgic Scott who was so upset when a number of reasonable reforms in the Scottish legal system were proposed, that he burst into tears while talking about them to Francis Jeffrey. 'He exclaimed, "No, no—'tis no laughing matter; little by little, whatever your wishes may be, you will destroy and undermine, until nothing of what makes Scotland Scotland will remain."'

'WAVERLEY'

By 1812 Scott's position as the best-selling poet of his day was being challenged. The young Lord Byron published the first cantos of *Childe Harold* in that year; when Scott brought out *Rokeby* in 1813, it was far less well received by the public. As Lockhart says, 'The deeper and darker passion of Childe Harold, the audacity of its morbid voluptuousness . . . had taken the general imagination by storm.' In the same year, a cold economic wind brought the Ballantyne printing business into real trouble. It was at this point that Scott turned to the writing of novels.

In 1805 he had commenced a novel called *Waverley*, but a friend to whom he had shown it had discouraged him. In 1810, he was searching an old desk for fishing-flies, and came across the forgotten manuscript. Ballantyne, however, doubted whether the novel would make much money. So Scott put it back again. It was not till 1813 that he got down to finishing it, in the hope that it would help his business out of difficulties; and then Constable offered only £700 for the copyright. In the summer of 1814 Scott gave a foretaste of what was to come, finishing the last two-thirds of the book in the evenings of three weeks at Edinburgh. One of the most astonishing episodes in the history of British publishing had begun.

2

Scott's Poetry and the Romantic Movement

'Romanticism' is best defined as the European cultural reaction to the French and Industrial Revolutions. This reaction could be right or left in its politics, but it was loaded with political awareness, and it was usually extreme. It encompassed Shelley's libertarian hopes of a magnificent future for humanity and Scott's wishful turning to the past. In music the response to fifty-odd years of turmoil could emerge in the light, sentimental touch of Donizetti or, later, in the sombre fulsomeness of Wagner. Poetry produced the simplicity of Blake's *Songs of Innocence* and the vaulting rhetoric of Victor Hugo; painting the heroic classicism of David, Constable's patient concern with appearances and the revolutionary formlessness of Turner. What the artists of Scott's lifetime shared was a shattering experience of politics, an experience that penetrated their life and outlook. It is over-simplifying but broadly true to say that by 1800 a wholly new attitude to nature, to life in nature, and to art in life was being born.

The principles of the 'mainstream' of 18th-century literature were founded on a narrow and unelevated idea of the function of the arts. Polite society was their proper environment, and there was little feeling that the artist should look elsewhere for inspiration or aspire beyond it. Literature was seen as the product of the accomplished gentleman's sensibility, the refinement of his understanding, not of inspired genius. The concept of the artist as genius, as the man apart from society, is romantic.

In Europe as a whole Romanticism found expression in every

art. In Britain we associate it chiefly with poets; with Blake and perhaps Burns, with Wordsworth and Coleridge and Southey, with Byron, Shelley and Keats. In discussing Scott as a poet we can place him in relation to the main currents of Romanticism.

SCOTTISH POETRY

One effect of the Age of Revolution was to encourage the rebirth of national literatures. In Italy, in Central Europe, in Scandinavia, Romanticism is associated with a new national self-consciousness. But Scott, for all his national pride and for all that he drew so much of his raw material from Scotland, is not truly a Scottish writer.

In the late 14th and early 15th centuries, under her Renaissance kings James IV and James V, Scotland had a language which, so far from being a mere English dialect, was an independent though allied tongue. Henryson, Dunbar, Gavin Douglas and David Lindsay produced a rich body of poetry—lyrical, narrative and dramatic. The Reformation and the union of the crowns thwarted the promise of a splendid national literature. Many cultural forces—including the adoption of the English translation of the Bible in Scotland—reduced Scots to the status of a dialect. In the 17th and early 18th centuries there were few literary works of any stature.

Yet, during Scott's own youth, Robert Burns had transcended the limitations of dialect and could have been seen as the herald of a rebirth of a truly Scottish poetry—not English verse written by Scotsmen but something truly independent. Scott could have chosen to write poems both in Scottish dialect and in conventional English, as Burns had done, or to risk writing only in the Scots which he habitually spoke himself.

We can see now that Scotland by the end of the 18th century was too completely integrated with England for such an enterprise to have been successful. But it remains significant that Scott never made a serious attempt to follow where Burns led. He wrote very few dialect poems, and these are late work, comic in tone and intention:

Donald Caird can drink a gill
Fast as hostler-wife can fill;
Ilka ane that sells gude liquor
Kens how Donald bends a bicker . . .

DONALD CAIRD'S COME AGAIN, 1818

This is doggerel jocularity and no more.

THE BALLADS

Scott's earliest poetic work is found in translations, striking and lively, of German romantic ballads written by sophisticated modern poets. It was in these mannered and lurid imitations, not in the original folk poetry of his own country, that Scott found his first inspiration.

Scott certainly enriched Scottish poetry by the editions of authentic ballads which he prepared (in some cases 'cooked up' would be the appropriate phrase) for *The Minstrelsy of the Scottish Border*. Scott, to quote Professor Hodgart, 'had little sense of editorial integrity; he could not resist the temptation to improve a ballad that came to him in an imperfect state. And the result is often very good poetry' (*The Ballads*, p. 111). We owe many standard anthology versions of the ballads to Scott—'The Wife of Usher's Well', 'The Twa Corbies' and 'Clerk Saunders' are examples. In the last case he changed the basis of the quatrain in which the ballad was found and his version does not fit any of its known tunes—a striking illustration of his lack of interest in music. 'The Twa Corbies' is probably Scott's original reshaping of a traditional ballad theme.

But his admittedly original ballads are remote from folk poetry. As an antiquarian Scott loved the ballads. As a gentleman, and as a poet, he condemned most of them for their 'rude and careless expression', for their 'loose and trivial composition', for their 'slovenly use of over-scutched phrases'; all of which were to be expected when they had been 'handed from one ignorant reciter to another' ('Introductory Remarks on Popular Poetry', *The Minstrelsy of the Scottish Border*, Volume 1).

So most of the 'ballads' which Scott invented to supplement *The Minstrelsy*, and those which are scattered through his lays and novels, are more or less typical examples of what amounted to a new literary form used by most of the Romantics. The 'literary ballad' rejects the rawness and the traditional ('over-scutched') phrases of folk poetry but uses its simple metres. It distils the medieval atmosphere and adds a sophisticated pathos and subjectivity which are alien to the true ballad. Other Romantic poets exploited elements of the ballads for their symbolic possibilities—most notably Coleridge in 'The Ancient Mariner'. Scott's original ballads, however, are either straightforward eerie tales ('The Eve of St. John') or emotional in a quite simple way.

'THE LAY OF THE LAST MINSTREL'

The ballad form could not convey a story in the modern style, with strongly individualised characters, romantic love and a critical attitude to violence. There are no individuals in the true ballads. Abrupt shifts from one situation to another rule out any exploration of complex motives. Cruelty, and also the supernatural, are taken for granted.

The ballads were only one of several influences on the series of lays on which Scott's reputation as an important poet must rest. Others were the metrical romances of the Middle Ages, and Spenser's *Faerie Queene*, which had delighted him in boyhood. When he launched seriously into poetry Scott turned naturally to narrative. But the ballads' irregular quatrains would have been impossibly monotonous for the large work which he planned. It was Coleridge's powerful unfinished narrative poem 'Christabel' which gave him a basis for *The Lay of the Last Minstrel*. Coleridge used couplets or quatrains (four lines of alternate rhymes) as it pleased him, arranging his verse in paragraphs of varying lengths and patterns. He counted the accents, not the syllables, in each line. There were always four accents, but the syllables varied from seven to twelve. This was the freedom Scott wanted, though he did not copy Coleridge exactly. The *Lay* is written with a suppleness which we find in none of its successors. Here is the description of the warders at Branksome Castle:

Ten of them were sheathed in steel,
With belted sword, and spur on heel:
They quitted not their harness bright,
Neither by day, nor yet by night:
  They lay down to rest,
  With corslet laced,
Pillow'd on buckler cold and hard;
  They carved at the meal
  With gloves of steel,
And drank the red wine through the helmet barr'd.

Canto I, Stanza 4

In this poem the varying lengths of the lines, and the wanderings of the stress within the lines, give constant interest, and even subtlety, to the texture of the verse. For this reason, although the story is crude and the characterisation mainly non-existent, good judges have preferred *The Last Minstrel* to the rest of Scott's copious poetic output.

'MARMION', 'THE LADY OF THE LAKE' AND 'ROKEBY'

Later he resorted increasingly to the octosyllabic couplet—only one of the many measures which he had used in *The Last Minstrel*. This made it easy for him to write—he engagingly admitted that its use 'encouraged' poets 'in a habit of slovenly composition'. It is the basic metre of *Marmion*, of *The Lady of the Lake* and of *Rokeby*. In *Marmion* he often varies it by throwing in a quatrain or some other pattern, and every lay includes a number of incidental songs in a great variety of shapes and metres. But after his first lay Scott gave up looking for freedom and subtlety and plumped for speed. He was, in fact, firmly set on the path which was to lead him to forsake poetry for the novel.

For the stories on which Scott framed his lays grew more complicated and interesting. In *The Last Minstrel* the Border violence and the melodramatic use of the supernatural make little serious claim on our sympathies. Only one character, William of Deloraine, is of much interest, and he is very simple compared to Scott's later rogues. In *Marmion*, however, the hero is a complex and vivid personality. Real events and historical figures are introduced—there is a striking portrait of James IV and a famous account of the Battle of Flodden. As Marmion casts his eye over the Scottish troops mustered at Edinburgh we see already Scott's interest in the social contrasts and clashes which were to be the stuff of his novels. Here are 'men at arms', 'young knights and squires', 'hardy burghers', yeomen, Borderers, and tribes of Highlanders—all Scotsmen indeed, but differently clad and armed, and with widely different attitudes to life. But the dignified conventions of narrative poetry which Scott had learnt from Spenser meant that he could not relate this briefly glimpsed spectrum of life to the fate of his hero.

In *The Lady of the Lake* there is a still wider range of striking characters. To a romantic love story Scott adds a historical theme, the same theme which he later handled in several novels—the contrast between the tribal life of the clans and the civil society of the Lowlands which threatened it.

The Middle Ages had so far served Scott for his stories. In *Rokeby*, his last important poem before *Waverley*, he turned to a later period, that of the English Civil War. The result was a lay which, while containing some of his best poetry, cried out to be a novel. The story is too involved and the characters too strong and varied to fit comfortably into a lay of Scott's usual length. Bertram of Risingham, the villain—or perhaps the hero?—is a very powerful creation. At exactly the moment when Byron's challenge to his popularity would in any case have prompted Scott to turn to prose, Scott had clearly exhausted the possibilities of the poetic lay. *The Bridal of Triermain* (1813) and *The Lord of the Isles* (1815) clearly show this exhaustion.

The lays are often slovenly in their execution. In pursuit of rhymes for his couplets, Scott will pervert grammar, slipping eelishly from one tense to another. And sometimes the rhymes themselves are out of place in serious verse ('O'er ptarmigan and venison/The priest had spoke his benison'). Scott remarked in *Rokeby*:

> 'Tis mine to tell an onward tale,
> Hurrying, as best I can, along,
> The hearers and the hasty song.

Canto 6, Stanza 26

And the clumsiness of those lines is all too typical of his 'hasty song'.

Furthermore the octosyllabic couplet is basically a blunt instrument. It easily creates the speed and flow which Scott wanted, and carries the reader on relentlessly. But there is very little scope for rhythmic variety within its narrow limits. As each line speeds breathlessly towards a thumping rhyme-word there is no time for subtleties of language.

In spite of this the lays are moving, exciting and surprisingly fresh. Their virtues are straightforwardness and frankness. Since these virtues are best revealed in contrast with other (and greater) poets, this is the point at which Scott's relationship to the Romantic movement may be defined.

SCOTT AND ROMANTICISM

An obvious characteristic of the Romantics (which must not, however, be over-emphasised at the expense of other features) was their interest in the supernatural. Unlike the calm philosophers of the 18th century they saw 'more things in heaven and earth' than could be explained by reason. Scott, true to his early interest in German ballads, infested his novels and poems with supernatural occurrences. But whereas Coleridge, for instance, uses the supernatural in his poetry for symbolic ends which make 'explanations' irrelevant, Scott is prone to present it apologetically, or to hint, in 18th-century fashion, that there must be some simple reason for the strangest happening.

The Romantics reacted violently and variously from the stilted diction and conventional forms of 18th-century poetry. Scott himself, in *The Last Minstrel* especially, concurred with Wordsworth and Coleridge in a zest for experiment. Like them, he sought freedom from cramping poetic regulations. In the rush of experiment many new forms were tried out. With this went a cult of spontaneity, which still affects our own attitude to literary creation. In Wordsworth's famous phrase, good poetry was 'the spontaneous overflow of powerful feelings'.

Scott's attitude to spontaneity is significant. In his 'Introduction to Canto Third' of *Marmion* he compares his verse to dappling clouds; to a stream which dashes down from the mountainside and then winds slowly across the plain; to autumn breezes which die away and then swell again:

> Thus various, my romantic theme
> Flits, winds, or sinks, a morning dream.
> Yet pleased, our eye pursues the trace
> Of Light and Shade's inconstant race;
> Pleased, views the rivulet afar,
> Weaving its maze irregular;
> And pleased, we listen as the breeze
> Heaves its wild sigh through Autumn trees;
> Then, wild as cloud, or stream, or gale,
> Flow on, flow unconfined, my Tale.

Just as the random effects of nature please the eye by their very fickleness, so readers should like a poet who lets himself go and pays little attention to formal regulations.

But the rest of the introduction, which is written as a letter to his friend Erskine, apologises for Scott's inability to do anything finer than let his fancy 'flow unconfined'. He confesses 'I love the licence all too well.' He cannot produce 'classic rhyme' like the masters of the 18th century. He explains that this is a result of his childhood in the Border country, which has made him 'ape the measure wild/Of tales that charmed me yet a child'. He can do no better, and appeals to his critical friend:

> On the wild hill
> Let the wild heath-bell flourish still;
> Cherish the tulip, prune the vine,
> But freely let the woodbine twine,
> And leave untrimm'd the eglantine.

(The disastrous quack of 'woodbine twine' makes us wish that Scott had confined his flow more often.)

So Scott *practised* spontaneity, but *preached* the doctrine that 'classic rhyme' was better. This attitude to poetry is consistent with his self-mocking view of his own novels, written equally freely, equally carelessly.

With the revolt against artificiality came a new attitude to nature. Again, Wordsworth is a key figure. In wild uncultivated country he saw, not a cause for fear or disgust, but positive signs of the grandeur of God. He praised mountains and cherished 'the meanest flower that blows'. Scott's practice clearly pointed in the same direction. He sets his first two lays in the Border hills, his third in the Highlands, his fourth in Northumberland. In *The Lady of the Lake*, King James pauses, 'raptured and amazed', over the wild scenery of Loch Katrine:

> High on the south, huge Benvenue
> Down on the lake in masses threw
> Crags, knolls and mounds, confusedly hurl'd,
> The fragments of an earlier world:
> A wildering forest feathered o'er
> His ruin'd sides and summit hoar,
> While on the north, through middle air,
> Ben-an heaved high his forehead bare.
>
> Canto I, Stanza 14

Words which, for Defoe, say, or Doctor Johnson, would have carried the worst of meanings—'confusedly hurl'd', 'wildering', 'ruin'd', 'bare'—are here used neutrally, and there is no doubt that Scott intends us to relish the scene which these adjectives describe.

Yet, as we shall see, this attitude is not so evident in the novels, where Scott, seriously concerned with human society, sees landscape from a utilitarian standpoint.

Wordsworth, besides exalting wild scenery, exalted the life of those closest to nature, the 'common people'. His aim in his *Lyrical Ballads* was 'to choose incidents and situations from common life' and to 'use a selection of language really spoken by men'. Scott rather snobbishly looked down on the 'ignorant reciters' of old ballads. Like Wordsworth he admired Burns, but he kept the common speech of his country out of his poetry. For him, common meant vulgar.

Yet, again, his practice was in key with 'the Spirit of the Age'. Indeed, of all the Romantics Scott, the Tory, was paradoxically the one who did most to bring the common people and the common life on to the stage of literature—not in his poetry but in his novels. Later we will say more about this, but we can quickly illustrate the contrast between Wordsworth's principles and Scott's practice. In 'The Solitary Reaper' Wordsworth pauses to contemplate a Highland lass singing as 'she cuts and binds the grain'. 'Will no one tell me what she sings?' asks Wordsworth, somewhat absurdly. Scott, of course, would have asked her, copied down the song, and had a friendly conversation with her.

Wordsworth's poem, though occasioned by a solitary girl, is really about Wordsworth's reaction to her. The common life, in this short lyric and in Wordsworth's long poem *The Prelude*, is important because Wordsworth sees it and admires it. This new emphasis on *subjectivity* is perhaps the most important of all the Romantic themes. Blake's impassioned prophecies, Keats's sensuality, Byron's barely disguised heroic poses, Shelley's overwhelming self-importance—the expression of the poet's personality was for the first time seen as an end in itself. Wordsworth thought his own mind so important that he wrote two huge poems about it, and projected a third. One might even say that Wordsworth in adoring nature was adoring himself, because he saw himself there all the time.

This was not mere blind egotism, of course. A lesson which the Romantics read from the French Revolution was that a perfect society was possible. The poet already represented a superior type of human nature. His development of his own powers, his expression of his own personality, was of importance for the whole of mankind.

Scott stood aside from all this. In his introductions to the cantos of *Marmion* he does, as we have seen, offer much analysis of his own development as a poet and of his own views of poetry—but he does so apologetically rather than self-assertively. Looking at his poetical works as a whole we can see that in this respect he was a reluctant romantic. The Oxford edition runs to 962 pages. In only a handful of unmemorable short lyrics does Scott write about his own feelings. The heroes of his lays are very obviously not projections of his own personality—as

Byron's heroes, equally obviously, were. Scott certainly had a very good conceit of himself, but he *did* veil his egotism, because he did not believe that he was himself an important subject for literature.

John Ruskin, the great Victorian art critic, was one of Scott's most enthusiastic admirers, and he puts his finger very accurately on this important contrast between Scott and his contemporaries. In the third volume of *Modern Painters* (1856) he contrasts the humility of Scott, and of Turner the great painter, with the egotism of Wordsworth:

> I do not find Scott talking about the dignity of literature, nor Turner about the dignity of painting. They do their work, feeling that they cannot well help it; the story must be told, and the effect put down; and if people like it, well and good; and, if not, the world will not be much the worse. Part IV, Chapter 16, Section 25

Ruskin goes on to contrast Scott's attitude to nature with that of other Romantic poets. Whereas Keats and Tennyson see nature as altered by their own feelings, Scott sees her as she is and enjoys her for her own sake. He

> follows her lead simply—does not venture to bring his own cares and thoughts into her pure and quiet presence—paints her in her simple and universal truth, adding no result of momentary passion or fancy, and appears, therefore, at first shallower than other poets, being in reality wider and healthier. 'What am I?' he says continually, 'that I should trouble this sincere nature with my thoughts. I happen to be feverish and depressed, and I could see a great many sad and strange things in those waves and flowers; but I have no business to see such things.' Section 37

Ruskin's whole chapter on Scott should be read; it contains perhaps the best criticism made of Scott as a poet.

So Scott, with his 'unconfined' flow, preserves a freshness which we can no longer find in Keats, or even in Wordsworth. Ruskin seizes on his essential virtue—his frank and unaffected attitude to his art, and to what he describes. With this goes a delight in variety—in variety of men, of places, of natural phenomena. Professor Donald Davie has described Scott's habit of piling up details as 'direct creative energy revelling in its own fecundity', and adds 'the copiousness of his invention is the greatest thing in Scott, in poetry and prose alike' (*Proceedings of the British Academy*, 1961).

The beginning of *Rokeby*'s final canto is a fine example of this 'copiousness of invention'. Scott shows us dusk falling in the Northumbrian woods. In fourteen lines he describes the creatures of the wood as they prepare for the night. The owl wakens, the bittern screams, the raven slumbers:

> Forth from his den the otter drew,—
> Grayling and trout their tyrant knew,
> As between reed and sage he peers,
> With fierce round snout and sharpen'd ears . . .

(The carelessness here is not noticed until one re-reads the passage; Scott slips from past to present as it suits his rhyme.) Then comes the hawk, sleeping after a day of watching doves 'dart across the dell'. Then we are reminded of a robber's cave in the woods, where we have seen Bertram plotting and carousing with his band. The 'copse and yew' on top of the crag throw 'dark shadows' on the river (Canto 6, Stanza 2).

Suddenly 'a solitary form' is noticed gliding through the wood. The owl sees him and is silent; the raven wakes and croaks; the otter hears him and dives. This is Edmund—a reluctant outlaw, now filled with remorse for his crimes.

In another poet of the time we might look for symbols in all these references to nature. But Scott, as Ruskin says, 'follows her lead simply'. If he wanted to symbolise Edward's guilt and repentance he could easily find something in the scene to suit him. Instead he conjures up the quiet of the wood, its glooms and glimpses of light, the abrupt noises of the animals. He creates a lifelike atmosphere. He is 'simply' describing a man walking through a wood at night.

Later, when Edmund is surprised by Bertram and seized, the latter remarks 'By heaven, he shakes as much/As partridge in the falcon's clutch'. For a moment we suspect that the glimpses of birds and beasts of prey *have* been symbolic of Bertram. Far from it—Bertram himself aids the young man in his good intentions and so helps bring about the marriage of hero and heroine. The image of the partridge is just one that has sprung to Scott's mind to describe the scene. And when Scott moralises on nature, as he does frequently, it is always a simple moral which he draws. At the opening of *Rokeby*'s third canto he contrasts a variety of animals and birds which prey on different species with man who 'turns the fierce pursuit on man'. It would be a misleading critic who tried to show that *Rokeby* was constructed round symbols of hunting. Scott is innocent of complicated symbolism, and means exactly what he says.

He creates his descriptions by sharp vivid flashes—like our sudden glimpse of the otter's snout. He paints a scene, as Ruskin points out, in bold colours:

> The *blackening* wave is edged with *white*;
> To inch and rock the seamews fly.
>
> LAST MINSTREL, Canto 6, Stanza 23

or combines colour with striking, easy similes:

> Old Barnard's towers are purple still,
> To those that gaze from Toller-hill;
> Distant and high, the tower of Bowes
> Like steel upon the anvil glows . . .
>
> ROKEBY, Canto 5, Stanza 1

But Scott, set down in the Rocky Mountains, could not have written effective nature poetry. The names of the peaks would have had no associations for him. The area itself had no history.

Nature for its own sake certainly meant a great deal to him. But he chose to write about it in relation to people. His best lays are set either in his Border Country, where every view and place-name had historical or personal associations for him, or in areas which he knew from visiting the country houses of friends, noblemen or gentlemen. (*Rokeby* is dedicated to the man who then owned Rokeby. When Fitzjames, in *The Lady of the Lake*, defeats the noble Roderick in single combat and rides furiously to Stirling, he passes several places where Scott's own friends lived.) In a sense, Scott is writing from personal feeling when he launches into one of his long lists of famous names or favourite places. But it is sentiment about his society, his nation, and its history, which inspires him; it concerns not him alone, but every living Scotsman.

SONGS

In the same way, the best of his short poems are not personal lyrics, but songs written for his characters in lay, novel or play. Scott's range of metres in these poems is enormous. He can manage the sentimental ballad style of 'O, Brignall banks are wild and fair', sung by Edmund in *Rokeby*, or the irresistible, swinging metre of 'Lochinvar' or 'Bonnie Dundee'. There is the rough, exciting marching song from *The Monastery*—

> March, march, Ettrick and Teviotdale,
> Why the deil dinna ye march forward in order?—

or the simple, moving courage of Major Bellenden's song in *Old Mortality*, perfectly suited to the old cavalier, who looks bravely towards death:

> For time will rust the brightest blade,
> And years will break the strongest bow;
> Was never wight so starkly made,
> But time and years would overthrow.

There are the unusual metres which he provides for his Highlanders to sing to—the beautiful 'Coronach' (funeral lament) in *The Lady of the Lake*, for instance:

> Fleet foot on the correi,
> Sage counsel in cumber,
> Red hand in the foray,
> How sound is thy slumber!
> Like the dew on the mountain,
> Like the foam on the river,
> Like the bubble on the fountain,
> Thou art gone, and for ever!

Many of these songs are regularly found in anthologies. Yet almost all of them lose a good deal when they are taken from their context. 'Lochinvar' is a simple-hearted little tale in isolation. But it has an ironical flavour in *Marmion*, where it is sung to James IV, notorious for his roving eye, by his current 'wily' mistress. She is flattering James, perhaps, by comparing him to Lochinvar—or teasing him, perhaps, since though he may be 'daring in love' and 'dauntless in war', he is certainly not 'faithful in love'.

Scott's most famous anthology-piece of all is 'Proud Maisie'. Almost every critic who spurns most of Scott's poetry goes on to add that this little ballad, at least, is 'perfect' or 'flawless'. Yet Scott himself quite certainly did not mean it to be perfect. Madge Wildfire, in *The Heart of Midlothian*, sings it as she dies (Chapter 40). We are told that the four verses which we are given are 'only a fragment or two' of the song which she sang, all that her hearers could pick out; and, as it is printed in the novel, gaps are clearly indicated after the second and third stanzas. Without these indications, read by itself, it is certainly a strange and effective 'literary ballad'. But read in its context it is moving in a far more direct way. The mad girl's vanity has often been illustrated during the novel. Now, in her last moments, she seems to half-understand her own foolishness, for 'proud' Maisie, doomed never to marry, is a distillation of her own personality.

PLAYS

Scott was certainly thinking of Shakespeare's Ophelia here. Like all the Romantics, he tried his hand at blank-verse drama. Like all of them, he failed to produce an actable play. *The Doom of Devoirgoil* is a lamentable combination of melodrama and farce. *Auchindrane* is an attempt at tragedy, with quite strongly-drawn characters, which would, however, be impossible to stage. Scott's most dramatic drama, indeed, was never intended for the stage. This is his two-act piece *Halidon Hill*, which deals with an imaginary battle between Scots and English. It has no plot in the usual sense, but the scenes between the contentious Scottish commanders have real suspense. Scott's blank verse, however, is irredeemably monotonous; he thumps heavily down on the last word of almost every line.

AN ASSESSMENT

While Scott's lays can still delight us, they are too careless to rank as great poetry. Scott's greatness rested in his grasp of character and in his understanding of history; he could express neither fully in his verse. Even his best songs are still better when we read them as coming from the mouths of his characters. This objectivity sets him apart from the other Romantics. Ruskin's remarks about his attitude to nature apply to a great extent to his attitude to people. As a novelist, he lets a wide range of characters speak for themselves. He even judges them by their own standards. He sets them in conflict, and describes the outcome. He has no 'message', except that people are like this, and that this is the way in which history works. He subordinates his own feelings to the reality of the history which he describes, whereas the other Romantics (to generalise broadly) are dedicated to the expression of their own ideas or personalities.

3

Scott and the Novel

The novel as a distinct form had not had a long life when Scott first turned to writing prose fiction in 1805. We usually take Defoe as Britain's first novelist and his *Robinson Crusoe*, published in 1719, as Britain's first novel, although of course the evolution of prose fiction had been more gradual than this. Defoe, in *Robinson Crusoe* and later in *Moll Flanders*, took prose narrative right away from allegory, from attempts to locate symbolic figures in a timeless and universal world, and wrote about contemporary adventure and about ordinary people firmly anchored in the contemporary scene. Of course, it remained part of the fiction-writer's business to make his characters' activities far from ordinary, but it was Defoe who brought this activity right on to his readers' doorstep. It is with him that we first begin to use the word 'realism' to describe the novelist's method. Defoe was trying to present as vividly as possible the real world as he saw, experienced and understood it. Until the emergence of the novel there had been no adequate literary form for dealing with reality in this kind of way. The novel had to be born: it fulfilled a genuine need for both writer and reader.

THE PROBLEM OF REALISM: SAMUEL RICHARDSON

Later 18th-century novelists were preoccupied with the problem of how to communicate their views of the contemporary scene in as real a way as possible. They had to make their version of reality lively and recognisable, yet be continually arranging and manipulating, interpreting and commenting. This was the first major problem in the novel's development. Although there were of course rich and creative conventions of characterisation and action in drama and epic poetry, conventions which the novel drew on right through the 19th century, the early novelists were for the most part establishing their own rules as they went. This, and their varied attempts to grapple with the problem of how to present and interpret reality, are what make the 18th-century novel so fascinating.

The three greatest fiction writers of the century, Richardson, Fielding and Sterne, each made very different attempts to solve this initial problem. These attempts were vital to the novel's growth, but by the time Scott was writing this had ceased to be the dominant challenge—or, at least, Scott himself did not recognise it as such. Scott approached his fiction in terms of a story to be told, of a theme to be worked out, of characters to be enjoyed. Richardson had two aims—to allow his readers to live minute by minute the lives of his central characters and to show his characters as conveyors of moral comment. In *Pamela* (1740), for example, he constructs the entire novel from letters supposedly written by the novel's heroine, often at moments of extreme excitement and danger, covering every minute of her life. No one could accept the method itself as being realistic. It meant that Pamela's pen hardly left the paper and that she was often writing under impossible circumstances. But it did mean that action was being translated into words with the greatest immediacy.

This kind of immediacy was important to the 18th-century novelists. Scott, on the other hand, deliberately chose to write about the past, to make it quite clear that he was relating events that had happened some time before. He often cast his novels in the frame of tales allegedly handed down by word of mouth. (This itself brought a different kind of immediacy, the closeness to events that continuity suggests.) He was cheerfully inconsistent in his position as omniscient author, often switching from being an acute observer of a scene to admitting that of course he could not describe all the details because it all happened a long time ago. Scott allowed himself to take every liberty as an author, and by this time the novel could stand such treatment. In fact the sometimes outrageous way in which he treated the form clearly injected it with new energy and scope.

HENRY FIELDING AND LAWRENCE STERNE

Scott made no rules for himself. Richardson did, and used these as a guide to realism. Fielding handled the interpretation of contemporary reality in a rather different way, and his method was partly influenced by an approach to reality which conflicted with Richardson's. Richardson was highly conventional in his moral stance, often more so than he himself would have been ready to admit. His morality is based on a rigid view of proper behaviour rather than on motive and genuineness of feeling. Fielding's view opposed this. Tom Jones, hero of the novel of that name, rollicks his way from woman to woman and tavern to tavern, yet he is generous and big-hearted and his real love for Sophia Western is not damaged. In Fielding's eyes Tom is more 'moral' than Richardson's virtuous but excitable Clarissa, heroine of his novel of the same name, who achieves heavenly bliss but little earthly comfort. Fielding comments directly on his novels' action, and thus makes his points very clear. Richardson at times implies a double standard, a dual comment: his characters themselves suggest one attitude, his own manipulation of them another. His kind of immediacy did not allow him direct comment. On the other hand, Fielding's intrusions at times confuse the novel's reality. The two novelists illustrate very clearly the difficulties that the novel faced at this stage. They also show that an essential characteristic of the novel as a separate form was that there could be no absolute rules for it. It came into existence partly to overcome the inevitable and appropriate restrictions of verse and in particular the rules and conventions of both prose and verse writing that the Augustan Age was forming.

Lawrence Sterne (1713–68) avoided the problems Fielding and Richardson had set themselves. His *Tristram Shandy*, published in nine volumes between 1759 and 1767, is a glorious concoction of anecdotes and reflections, the tone of which is determined by the wandering mind and eccentric personality of Tristram himself. There is no chronological development, no pattern and no logical relationship in Tristram's narrative. The result is a thoroughly subversive piece of fiction. It seemed that Sterne had ditched the problem of how to present reality altogether. In fact, he found a solution which was not to be experimented with again for 150 years—he presented the contemporary scene entirely through the mind of a single character. Again, the problem which Sterne solved did not worry Scott a great deal. He moved in and out of his characters' minds at will, using them as vehicles of interpretation when he wished, abandoning them when this was no longer necessary. But he was sometimes self-conscious about this. He took fuller advantage than any previous writer of the author's omniscient position but he sometimes felt that he had to apologise for the liberties he took. It was not until the 20th century that the novelist was able to remove himself entirely from his own narrative without having recourse either to letters or to the first person as a technique of story-telling.

THE GROWTH OF THE NOVEL

The novel as a form developed very rapidly throughout the century. But by 1740 novels were being published at the rate of only seven a year. By 1770 about twenty novels a year were being published. We cannot make sense of figures like these without some understanding of the way the reading public was growing. The novel had an immediate appeal, particularly to the middle-class lady who found her leisure increasing as the industrial manufacturing of commodities grew, and was looking for ways of amusing herself. It was becoming more usual for the daughters of the household to occupy their mornings with useful reading—and this included novels, for it long remained frowned upon for a young lady to indulge in more intellectual pursuits—whereas before they would have concerned themselves with household tasks. Throughout the period, and while Scott was writing, the reading public was largely feminine. Eric Hobsbawm says, in his book *The Age of Revolution*, 'Romanticism entered middle-class culture perhaps mostly through the rise in day-dreaming among female members of the bourgeois family'.

Prose fiction fed the imaginations of this growing readership. The novel itself was a product of middle-class energy and its readers were in the early stages almost entirely so. It was not until later that the growing literacy of the working class and the wider availability of books brought a dramatic increase in sales figures and a wider variety of public demand.

A crucial factor in this increase was the beginning of the circulating libraries. 1740 saw the first of these in London. For a small annual membership fee readers were able to borrow books at a penny or so per volume. Novels were usually published in three volumes, and by the time *Waverley* appeared the usual price was one guinea. The circulating libraries spread rapidly and began to attract a new kind of reader. The serving maid sent to fetch the latest novel for her mistress often could not resist having a read herself. With the Industrial Revolution the population was growing fast. The working class, content until now with chapbooks and broadsheets for their literary entertainment, began to turn to the novel as it became more easily available. The tiny reading public of the early years of the century had by its close grown phenomenally, and this, inevitably, had its effects on the quality of the novels produced.

In the last thirty years of the century about forty novels were being published a year. In modern terms this seems an insignificant figure. But when we remember the population of the time—nine million in 1801 when the first census was taken—the literacy of the population and the limited leisure it had for reading, we can see the figure in its true perspective. During the novel's early life it was perhaps moulded as much by public taste and demand as by the deliberate experiments of the authors themselves. As the demand for fiction grew and the circulating libraries spread, the increasing number of novels published inevitably included a large amount of second-rate writing. Just as the bulk of the reading public was female, by the end of the century there were numbers of woman writers who seemed to have turned to the writing of fiction because they had little better to do. They recognised what the public wanted and they produced it. Of course, not all the woman writers were undistinguished. Mrs. Radcliffe, Fanny Burney, Maria Edgeworth and, supremely, Jane Austen in their own different ways handled the new form with sensitive skill.

THE GOTHIC ROMANCE

Many of the women novelists came in on the tidal wave of Gothic romance. In 1765 Horace Walpole (1717–97) published his *The Castle of Otranto*, and this was the beginning of a kind of fiction that was to dominate the drawing-rooms until Scott himself to some extent supplanted it. The 'Gothic' novel, the tale of horror and mystery superficially based on the medieval and crammed full of spine-chilling episodes spiced with doomed romance, seized hold of wilted middle-class imaginations. *The Castle of Otranto* never lets up for a single paragraph, and if we now find the book shapeless and boring we must at least acknowledge Walpole's incredible inventiveness as he moves breathlessly from incident to incident. The denizens of the drawing-room would indeed have gasped with horror at every page, and then asked for more. More was provided, and the Gothic novel flooded the market for something like fifty years.

Perhaps the two most famous—and best—Gothic novels are Mrs. Radcliffe's (1764–1823) *The Mysteries of Udolpho* (1794) and Matthew Lewis's (1775–1818) *The Monk* (1796). Both these writers had genuine ability in the way they manipulated the standard ingredients of Gothic. They were no more credible or authentic than the others, but there was an energy that produced something more than incident after incident formlessly tacked together. Mrs. Radcliffe handled characterisation with some skill and credibility, and shaped her novels carefully.

Scott, long before he himself began to write fiction, had kept up with the contemporary novel. On his desk there was usually to be found a pile of the most recent works of fiction. He was a great admirer of (and knew personally) Matt Lewis, and he certainly read and absorbed the same novels that his own future readers were enjoying. In an article in *The Quarterly Review* Scott ironically described the experience of reading through a batch of the latest in Gothic:

> We strolled through a variety of castles, each of which was regularly called Il Castello; met with as many captains of *condottieri*; heard various ejaculations of Santa Maria or Diavolo; read by a decaying lamp in a tapestried chamber dozens of legends as stupid as the main history, examined such suites of deserted apartments as might fit up a reasonable barrack; and saw as many glimmering lights as would make a respectable illumination.

Scott provides us here with a convenient list of some of the essentials of the Gothic novel. But in spite of his irony he himself did not scorn to introduce glimmering lights and deserted apartments into his narratives. Although usually he handled such elements of the Gothic as he did use with less superficiality and more skill than the producers of standard Gothic he could at times be as heavy handed as those he criticised. But however he handled them, it is quite clear that he enjoyed them, and that he was intrigued by the possibilities of mystery and the supernatural.

In the 1790s the novel received another fillip. It was then that the Minerva Press was set up by one William Lane, who devoted his business to the production of a steady stream of romances, Gothic and otherwise. The public lapped up the picturesque, whether entirely fanciful or vaguely realistic, whether it was picturesque horror or picturesque romance. It seemed to want something to challenge its imagination—'the colossal, the impassioned, the dark sublime'. But we must not think of the Gothic as an aberration in the development of the novel. It had important features that were very relevant to Scott's fiction and to later 19th-century writers.

The heroes of these tales are outside the picturesque. They are accomplished 18th-century gentlemen who behave according to 18th-century decorum rather than in response to Gothic situations. In this way they resemble Scott's heroes—his first, Edward Waverley, is a prime example—who come from outside the area of action and have little influence on it. Perhaps more significant is the fact that the origins of the Gothic tale and the origins of the historical romance are virtually inseparable. The historical novel as it existed before Scott was a transplanting of

18th-century heroes and heroines and behaviour into a vaguely medieval background that was more colourful than authentic. History simply provided a means of painting the 18th century in more exotic colours than the contemporary scene allowed—or than superficial observation of the contemporary scene yielded. Scott's novels are *about* history. Even at their crudest and least authentic they have a grasp of the movement and meaning of history which is, in the truest sense, revolutionary.

FANNY BURNEY AND JANE AUSTEN

At the same time as the Gothic was flooding the drawing-rooms and the Minerva Press was introducing the novel to factory hands and servant girls, writers like Fanny Burney and Jane Austen were making a more sophisticated impact. The novel with a contemporary setting had become much narrower in scope since *Tom Jones* or the works of Tobias Smollett (1721–71), a Scottish writer who lived in England and wrote wide-ranging novels, often crude but always lively. Fanny Burney (1752–1840) really belonged to the pre-Minerva Press days, for although she was still writing well into the 19th century she was by that time regarded as rather old-fashioned. Her first novel, *Evelina*, was published in 1778 and it contains a much more intimate and restricted observation of society than wider-ranging novels allowed. Fanny Burney's appeal was definitely to the pre-Minerva Press public, above rather than below stairs, but even so she was very widely popular, and read by statesmen and members of the royal household.

Jane Austen (1775–1817) was less lucky with her public. She had only published two novels, *Sense and Sensibility* in 1811 and *Pride and Prejudice* in 1813 before Scott swept in with *Waverley*. Few of her readers recognised her true worth, and while Fanny Burney's *Camilla* was ostentatiously displayed in fashionable dwellings, *Pride and Prejudice* was put away on a side table along with the products of the Minerva Press. Jane Austen's observation of a tiny section of society is penetrating and ironic, and although one can criticise her for what seems to be a complete unawareness of the world outside, of the devastating influence of public events—the Napoleonic Wars, for instance—this does not detract from her delicate and witty brilliance. Jane Austen and Scott were writing at the same time, but while she was narrowing and refining the content of the novel he was throwing into it anything he could find from his own experience, his own reading, from history, from the life of Edinburgh, of the Borders and the Highlands, and of course from his own irrepressible imagination. One of the delights of Scott's novels is precisely that they are unrefined and unpolished. They are full of raw material which Scott brings into the fold of art without damaging its natural strength. Jane Austen carefully selected and finely formed the ingredients of her novels, and while Scott's wit warms and rounds his characters Jane Austen's sharpens and refines.

MARIA EDGEWORTH AND THE REGIONAL NOVEL

There was another woman writer who often lay unappreciated in the corner of the drawing-room, a writer whom Scott much admired and to whom he warmly acknowledged a great debt. This was Maria Edgeworth (1767–1849). Maria Edgeworth was the first to make the locality, characters and customs of a particular region the subject of her novels. She was also one of the first 'social novelists' in the sense that she laid great emphasis on the conditions of life of all classes. She was less interested in manners than in the details of everyday living. In *Castle Rackrent* (1800) for instance she writes about decaying Irish gentry through the eyes of an ancient loyal serving-man whose position as a bridge between two classes and unsophisticated but canny outlook colour the narrative in a way that was new in British fiction. Scott describes some of Maria Edgeworth's qualities and shows what he owed to her when he says this in the General Preface to the complete edition of the *Waverley* novels:

> Without being so presumptuous as to hope to emulate the rich humour, pathetic tenderness, and admirable tact, which pervade the works of my accomplished friend, I felt that something might be attempted for my own country, of the same kind with that which Miss Edgeworth so fortunately achieved for Ireland—something which might introduce her natives to those of the sister kingdom,

in a more favourable light than they had been placed hitherto, and tend to procure sympathy for their virtues and indulgence for their foibles.

Maria Edgeworth interpreted the Irish scene to the English reader, and Scott hoped to do the same for Scotland. But while the Irish novels were neither widely read nor their importance understood, the novels that made the journey by sea from Edinburgh to London were adored by a huge public. And if this public was not conscious of what Scott was doing for Scotland it could not help absorbing his message.

THE NOVEL IN SCOTLAND

The Scottish novel as such had little solid existence before Scott himself virtually invented it. There had, of course, been Scottish novelists. Smollett in the mid-18th century, although he did not live in Scotland itself, gave many of his characters Scottish origins and connections with his native country. A Scottish novelist of a very different kind, whom Scott knew and admired, was Henry Mackenzie (1745–1831). Through most of Scott's adult life he was the grand old man of Scottish literature. His *Man of Feeling* (1771) was the ultimate in the novel of sentiment, a form which had its origins in France but was widely imitated—and popular—in Britain. This is fiction created out of a distilled sentimentalism in which feeling and simplicity for their own sake are the highest virtues. Mackenzie's man of feeling tenderly weeps his way through a series of heart-rending incidents and is upheld as a supreme moral example. The fact that he is a Scot, and comes from and returns to Scotland, has little importance in the novel.

At a time when the cultured society of Edinburgh was trying to shed its Scottish accent and remove all traces of dialect from its writing, Scott deliberately sat down to write about Scotland and Scottish people as he saw and heard them. He had from his boyhood been an avid reader—he described himself as 'a glutton of books'. He had a phenomenal memory, and the result was that books he read in his youth were as likely to have influenced him in some way as those he read in middle age. His first attempt at fiction was 'in the style of the Castle of Otranto, with plenty of Border characters, and supernatural incident'. But though he was a great reader of fiction the influences on his own work were as likely—perhaps more likely—to come from Shakespeare and Ben Jonson, of whom he was also an early reader, as from his immediate predecessors. It was some years after the Otranto experiment that it became clear to Scott that a more natural subject for fiction was Scotland itself. His knowledge of the Highlands and the talks he had had with the veterans of 1745 suggested to him 'that the ancient traditions and high spirits of a people, who, living in a civilised age and country, retained so strong a tincture of manners belonging to an earlier period of society, must afford a subject favourable for romance, if it should not prove a curious tale marred in the telling'.

'WAVERLEY'

This was the beginning of *Waverley*. Edward Waverley, full of romantic notions but with little experience of life, finds himself through personal affections and loyalties in the midst of the '45 Rebellion. He is English and a political innocent, he has had both Whig and Tory influences in his upbringing, but these have been remote or vaguely articulated, and his attitude to the Cause has an objectivity born of ignorance and lack of immediate contact. But he is also an ordinary, commonsensical and attractive young man of good breeding who finds that his experience of the clans both supports and contradicts the romantic ideas his 'desultory' education had fed him with. His personal involvement with those who support the Rebellion is encouraged by a natural curiosity in what is to him a completely new world. But the fact that he is a gentleman and does not act passionately saves him from the ruthlessness of history.

Edward Waverley is the link between the wild Highlands of 1745 and the tame drawing-rooms of sixty years later. He is a young man whom any of Scott's readers would have been happy to entertain. He is also a 'man of feeling', not so prone to tears as Mackenzie's, but sympathetic and sensitive though not very self-aware, and with a natural understanding of gentlemanly behaviour. If as a romantic he is devastated by the loss of Flora MacIvor, the passionately committed sister of a Jacobite chieftain, as a gentleman he is happy with the love of Rose Bradwardine and her simple and unsophisticated loyalty. This was Waverley's passport to polite society. The Highlands, the clans and the Rebellion were the novel's passport to an immense public.

Scott published *Waverley* anonymously. There seem to have been a variety of reasons for this, one being that he was fearful of damaging the reputation he had already made as a poet. But whatever the dominant reason, the mystery of the novel's authorship added to its popularity, and Scott quickly realised this. Novels continued to issue from his pen as from 'the Author of *Waverley*'. It was not until 1828 that he publicly confessed his responsibility for them, though his friends and most of Edinburgh had guessed years before this.

In the summer of 1814 *Waverley* was published. The Napoleonic Wars were temporarily over and there was a general feeling of optimism, a feeling that it was time to move on to new things. The reading public was sated with the Gothic. It had loved Scott's poetry, though *Rokeby* was not selling well; it was lapping up Byron but paying little regard to Miss Austen's *Mansfield Park*. It was ready for something new, and *Waverley* seemed to be the answer.

The first edition of one thousand was sold out in five weeks. The book's fame spread rapidly to London where it was quickly taken to the hearts of fashionable society. It was read by the Prince Regent himself. John Murray recommended the book to his wife in this way: 'Pray read *Waverley*, it is excellent. No dark passages; no secret chambers; no wind howling in long galleries.' Maria Edgeworth, who guessed the author at once, was unequivocal in her praise. 'I am more delighted with it than I can tell you; it is a work of first-rate genius,' she wrote to John Ballantyne (James's brother, who collaborated in the printing press). In fact, *Waverley* made a stunning impact, and although Scott's popularity was to fluctuate considerably over the eighteen fiction-writing years of his life he never entirely lost this hold over the public's imagination.

SCOTT'S POPULARITY

Why was Scott so popular? Though Hazlitt, another admirer, remarked that 'If put to the vote of all the milliner's girls in London *Old Mortality* or even *The Heart of Midlothian* would not carry the day (or at least not very triumphantly) over a common Minerva Press novel', the author of *Waverley* became a household word in almost every section of society. Part of the explanation has already been suggested. Novel readers, and the novel itself, were ready for something new. Scott, with his intimate knowledge of the contemporary novel, certainly understood this. Whether he could have provided new scope for the novel without the particular circumstances of his own life, is another matter.

The public clearly wanted heroics and romance, but they also wanted a means of identifying with the novel's content. Scott's ordinary unheroic heroes led his readers into an area of heroic action and picturesque location. The action was historical and the location actual. Edward Waverley behaves with magnanimity and good breeding under circumstances that transform such behaviour into heroism—his rescue of Colonel Talbot, the English officer, from the wrath of the Jacobites for whom Waverley is fighting, for example. In saving an enemy officer from death Waverley is both hero and pragmatist—he is acting usefully for his own good. He behaves with spontaneous generosity and safeguards his own future, for later Colonel Talbot responds by saving Waverley from the grim fate of most of the captured Jacobites. Scott's well-bred, uncommitted heroes are one of his novels' most characteristic features and it is appropriate that Waverley, his first, should be his most perfect example. His characteristic hero lives right through his fiction, not because Scott had found a successful formula and simply repeated it, but because such a hero provided for the contemporary reader a convenient means of approaching history, of making sense of opposing historical forces, between which it was impossible to make a moral choice.

The full explanation of Scott's popularity is more complicated and less tangible than this. But it has to be remembered that Scott was a historical novelist, writing about history at a time when the shattering events of the French Revolution had shocked men, including Scott, into a new awareness of the past. In his book *The Historical Novel* Georg Lukacz shows how the wars in Europe that followed the French Revolution had brought something new to men's awareness of themselves in history and as part of a nation. It became necessary to propagandise war as an activity for the sake of the well-being of individuals as well as governments. The mass conscript armies that lurched across Europe had to be convinced that they were fighting for issues with which they themselves were involved. If they did not realise that they were making history, they began to understand that the past had a great deal to do with the present. It was this new awareness that Scott seized hold of, perhaps unconscious of what he was doing. He presented through his novels a new kind of interest in the past, and a new kind of response to the historical process. He became preoccupied with how and why society had arrived where it had at the time he was writing.

The appeal of Scott's history was probably not recognised in this way by his readers. Nevertheless it satisfied a genuine need, a need that ran right down through the classes. It satisfied also a restlessness in Scott himself, which we are aware of all through his writing and the activities of his life. He felt the necessity of making the attempt to sort out the contradictory forces in the Scotland of his own day. His interests and his occupations, his daily life, his friends all helped to keep this necessity alive. And always he had before him Edinburgh itself as a reminder of both the continuity of history and the jolting shocks of progress.

4

The Waverley Novels

The friends to whom Scott had shown the early chapters of *Waverley* had pronounced them dull. On publication the novel was an instant success, but it is certainly the case that the reader of Scott has to be prepared to cover a great deal of ground in mere preliminaries to the action. There are reasons for this. In *Waverley* there are several chapters devoted to Edward's background and upbringing; his romantic tendencies and his neutral position are both crucial to the novel. It was important both to Scott's idea of character and to his historical grasp of his subject that this kind of detail should be filled in. This does not necessarily mean that the earlier parts of all his novels had to be slow moving. In fact, many of them begin right in the middle of things—*Old Mortality*, for instance, or *The Heart of Midlothian*. The latter in particular begins with an explosive incident—the Porteous Riots—which is central in the novel and launches us straight into the novel's action and meaning. But this technique could not always be used. It was only when his subject yielded suitable material, material that could be used with reference both to character and theme, that Scott could apply such a technique of opening his narrative. In *Waverley* he begins with the man and not the event. The civilised gentleman wrestles with the untamed drama of action. In *The Heart of Midlothian* it is as if the events threw up the characters, as if the Porteous Riots were a small volcano. These are two parts of the movement of history.

Four months after the publication of *Waverley*, Scott began *Guy Mannering*. He wrote it in six weeks, and it was published in February 1815. Thus began the great river of fiction that was to pour from his pen over the next seventeen years, a number of years seeing the publication of more than one novel, not to mention prose works of other kinds. And all the time he was writing Scott continued to fulfil his duties as Sheriff, and at the Court in Edinburgh, led a very full social life, entertained continuously at both Abbotsford and Castle Street, and found time for all his outdoor activities also. He continued his strict routine of writing early in the morning. He rarely allowed this to be interrupted. Even when he was ill, as he increasingly was, or depressed with financial problems, he continued to write. In fact he says in his Journal that the rare occasions when he felt completely disinclined to write were a sign that he was completely relaxed.

THE SCOTTISH NOVELS

Scott's first nine novels were all set in Scotland. His own background, his feeling of being in touch with history through the tales of the Border and the memories of the generation before him who had lived at a time when war was still a traditional way of life in Scotland, provided his richest source of material. This was supplemented by the variety of his reading. Scott still felt the power of the recent past over the present, although at the same time he was troubled by the signs of the present getting out of control, and for him the recent past stretched back to the days of the Covenanters. The past seemed to him both a natural subject for his pen and a subject with which it was necessary to come to grips. His fellow Scots recognised the need also, and it was largely for this that the cultured society of Edinburgh read his novels.

Like *Waverley*, *Guy Mannering* begins with an intrusion, the intrusion of a 'young English gentleman' into Galloway. Guy Mannering's difficulties in the first pages, his inability to understand or make himself understood by the people of Galloway, introduce the novel's major theme. Though the plot is one of mystery and intrigue and the characters illustrations of manners rather than of historical forces, the novel is about encroachment. It shows what happens when outsiders encroach upon the life of this tiny area of Scotland, when they come into association and conflict with the people who know no other life than that they have always lived, and whose standards are local rather than those of polite society. There is no rich historical conflict here, but a variety of social disruptions on every kind of level. In most of the Scottish novels we have both, the major conflict and the smaller upheavals in the lives of ordinary people that are in fact reflections of this conflict. We shall see that this is one of the most important features of Scott's novels. The daily sufferings of insignificant people balance the large-scale defeats and victories of great men. Small-scale squalor confronts widespread destruction. Death by deprivation exists side by side with the grand execution. Perhaps of all Scott's qualities his sense of proportion is his most impressive.

The theme of the intruder is a basic one in all of Scott's novels, but we see it most clearly related to the historical themes in this group of Scottish novels. It is not so much present in *The Antiquary*, which followed *Guy Mannering*, for the intrusive hero has so little to do with the novel's vitality, but we see it as a key to the historic process in *Old Mortality*, published in 1816 with *The Black Dwarf*, and in *Rob Roy* and *The Heart of Midlothian*, both published in 1818. Scott turned to the past in order to explain the present. In doing so he tried to provide as many leads to the present as he could. He had to guide the imagination of his own day, the mind of civilised Edinburgh and its growing self-confidence and commitment to progress, in the strangeness of a past that for most people was virtually dead. The cunning daring of the Macgregors, the romantic heroism of the MacIvors, had no place in the civilisation of the early 19th century. In approaching history by following the lead of well-bred gentlemen with 19th-century manners, Scott was using the experience of his own readers as a way into unknown territory.

The Antiquary combines a plot whose melodramatic heights coincide with its comic fulfilment with an underlying seriousness which is frequently not recognised. This novel is often dismissed as slight, if entertaining, but in fact the very incongruity of its ingredients demands serious attention. Action and characters are

Abbotsford

'The craigs of Arthur's Seat, and the sea coming in ayont them. . . .'— 'Edinburgh' from the South, at the time of Scott's death, by Joseph Turner

'The Tower of Wolf's Crag', by H. Melville—Scott the Romantic, as his contemporaries saw the novels

Scott's favourite portrait of 'Bonnie Dundee'. 'And there was Claverhouse, beautiful as when he lived. . . .' *Redgauntlet*, Letter XI continually balanced between the comic, the tragic and the pathetic, and Scott's skill is such that he can vary depth and intensity without losing sight of any of these elements. Jonathan Oldbuck, the antiquary, links the ridiculous villain Dousterswivel and the tragic courage of the Mucklebackits with a kind of muddle-headed shrewdness. If there is no major clash there are ripples of conflict which make up a solid texture of social comment.

But it is in *Old Mortality* that the pattern of *Waverley* is caught up again. Henry Morton, rationally determined not to get involved in political or religious troubles, is forced to make a choice. Like Edward Waverley and so many of Scott's other heroes he has to decide whether to back out quickly from the action where his natural humane sympathies have led him or whether to complete his involvement by committing himself wholeheartedly. He does the latter, fights in the Covenanters' battles, but remains an outsider because he can never abandon himself to extremity. In other words he keeps his objectivity and his good breeding, so that, when the battles are over and he has paid the price of action, he is able to lead a normal life that is not disturbed by the consequences of events. He suffers, but not in the long run. He pays a price, but one that his youth and gentlemanliness can afford.

In *Rob Roy* Frank Osbaldistone hardly has the chance to make any decisions. His association with Rob Roy Macgregor is forced on him, and his understanding of what is happening is far behind the events themselves. Here, though, there is a factor that we have to take more seriously than in many of Scott's novels. Henry Morton's attachment to Edith Bellenden is not an important part of the essential action of *Old Mortality*. But Frank is led into deeper and deeper water by his growing affection for Di Vernon, who has a unique place amongst Scott's heroines. She is the most attractive and the most active of his female characters. She is also a vital link in the plot itself, alert, tantalising, but above all with an understanding of events that Frank does not gain until the novel's end.

Frank, the innocent lad from the metropolis, stumbles blindly into Macgregor country. The intrusion works the other way in *The Heart of Midlothian*. It also has a rather different function. Instead of the neutral gentleman being temporarily overwhelmed by the force of events, the humble Jeanie Deans confronts the Court (and is hardly aware that it is a confrontation) and conquers simply by being herself. Already we can see that, although *Waverley* provides so many clues to our understanding of Scott's novels, there is great variety in the way the pattern is arranged. Scott's purpose in this first group of novels is in general always the same. Even some of his characters are in general the same. But the events themselves, the particular points in time and place that determine the character of the novel, are different in each case.

In *The Heart of Midlothian* there is confrontation not in terms of battles and beliefs but in terms of class, character and ethical standards. Scott dispenses with leading lines to the present and comes close to allowing history to speak for itself, or at least to speak through the mouths of historical characters rather than neutral observers. Here the neutral characters, Reuben Butler, for instance, are the weak characters. It is the characters through whom social and ethical forces are solidly represented, Jeanie herself, the Duke of Argyle, that contain the novel's strength.

The two short novels that round off this phase, *The Bride of Lammermoor* and *The Legend of Montrose*, published together in 1819, do not fit into the *Waverley* pattern at all. They are curiously combined for they differ greatly from each other. *The Bride of Lammermoor* is unrelenting and very powerful tragedy with a stark, bleak atmosphere that is quite different from anything one finds in any other of Scott's novels. This must be partially due to the fact that Scott wrote it at a time when he was so ill that afterwards he could not recall a word of what he had written. But there is no flaw that one can particularly attribute to this. Details of background and characterisation are handled with a brief economy that we rarely find in Scott. This gives the book much of its unusual character. Events have a suddenness, a swiftness, which we feel is quite out of the control of the characters involved.

Here the intrusion is more like a flood. Instead of a single character penetrating unknown territory, civilisation swallows up an old world. The dark, defensive Ravenswood retreats into his lonely dilapidated castle but finds no refuge from the encroachment of progress. The fate that legend has spelt out for the last of the Ravenswoods is also that of the old life. Also swallowed up in the flood is Lucy Ashton, who, through her love for Ravenswood, turns from the new world her father has helped to make to the old world he is helping to destroy. She, perhaps, is the real equivalent of Waverley, but being a woman and helpless in the grip of others she has no hope of surviving the ordeal. Flora MacIvor's rejection of Waverley saves him from the consequences of Jacobitism. Ravenswood's final insistence on his love for Lucy when she is irrevocably promised to the eligible Bucklaw destroys her.

In *The Legend of Montrose* the tone, the process, everything is reversed. The irresistibly comic and breathtakingly egocentric personality of Dugald Dalgetty transforms reality. The book's atmosphere and its historical detail are far from authentic, but Dalgetty influences our reaction to such an extent that we forget the rather large quantity of totally improbable detail. Dalgetty is an admirably successful intruder because he refuses to succumb to the conventional (and outdated) attitudes towards how the gentleman soldier ought to behave. He cannot be called brave, yet he is completely without fear because fear would come between him and his job, his money-making. He cannot be criticised for his idiocies and egotism because he does his job well and the officers he serves come to rely on him.

Dalgetty is a comic antithesis of the doubtful Waverley, impressed yet worried by his experiences, but *The Legend of Montrose* illustrates a clash on the same lines as that we find in *Waverley*. Dalgetty, the modern soldier, has outlived heroism, has outlived causes, just as Waverley's civilisation has, but Dalgetty's loyalty can be bought and sold, and although he is a product of the modern age—or perhaps because of this—he has not the breeding and sensitivity that make Edward Waverley and Henry Morton such admirable representatives of civilisation.

Yet Dalgetty triumphs, while Waverley and Morton have to retreat.

Dugald Dalgetty is Scott's only comic hero, but Scott's comic characters are a very important feature of his novels. None of this first group of nine, even *The Bride of Lammermoor*, is without its comedy. And we can see emerging in the Scottish novels several distinct types of comic and partly comic characters who reappear in various guises right through Scott's fiction. The comedy is sometimes there for the sheer fun of it, but usually it is full of purpose. The 'faithful follower' type, for instance—Cuddie Headrigg in *Old Mortality* or Andrew Fairservice in *Rob Roy*—is an essential link between the humourless hero and the rougher humanity he encounters. The comic character breaks down the barriers—our barriers as well as the hero's—and precipitates us more vigorously into the life of the novel than the hero's polite gestures can manage. And although most of Scott's richest comedy is in the Scottish novels, or novels which contain Scottish characters, none of his novels are without it.

Many of Scott's comic types—the pedant, the sot, the rake—appear again and again. But, if he uses the same techniques and draws continually on familiar material, the results are always different. We can grow weary of Scott's wavering plots and clumsy construction, but never of this gallery of characters whom he conjures out of the soil, the straggling Highland villages, the dark Edinburgh tenements, and decaying ancestral homes. Every class and every condition is fertile in this respect. There are other types, too, that we quickly come to recognise as we read Scott's novels, more serious, even tragic characters. Edward Waverley provides the model for most of Scott's heroes. The outcast—the gipsy, the beggar, the socially unacceptable—who very often has some secret knowledge of the past or understanding of events that the main characters are without, recurs again and again. Edie Ochiltree, the beggar in *The Antiquary*, is almost a comic character. His laconic independence and superior knowledge carry him beyond misery. But Madge Wildfire, the deranged wanderer in *The Heart of Midlothian*, is deeply disturbing, and Meg Merrilies, the gipsy in *Guy Mannering*, bears her knowledge with a dignified and tragic sense of loss. These characters remind us of the savagery and desolation which never seriously mark the heroes.

There is another kind of semi-comic character who reminds us of a side of life equally important. Dandie Dinmont in *Guy Mannering* is an example. He illustrates another meaning of the word gentleman. Bertram recovers his lost heritage—his name, his status and his property. But Dandie's inheritance is the Border country of Liddesdale, his name and status have meaning only through his own character and actions, and his property is useful only in so far as he makes it so. Although Scott placed so much importance on the idea of the well-bred gentleman of property with good, preferably aristocratic, blood in his veins, the humbly born, commonsensical, kind, good-humoured Dandie Dinmont was also for him a model of what man should be. The combination of natural canniness and natural kindness marks many of Scott's most impressive characters.

SCOTT'S SENSE OF BALANCE

We can see this same combination in Scott himself. His novels reveal his personality to some extent, but not so strikingly and movingly as his Journal, which he began to keep in 1825 at a time when his life was at its most difficult. Scott was a Tory, he believed in upholding tradition, but above all he was humane, and it is this quality that illuminates his novels. His comedy is never vicious, his condemnations never without some saving mark of appreciation for the man involved. Although his political sympathies are always clear, he is neither dogmatic nor blinded in his approach to the other side. This superb sense of balance is another factor which helps to explain his popularity.

THE HISTORICAL ROMANCES

In 1815, with two novels published, Scott made a trip to London, and although he officially denied authorship of the novels, London society received him as their author. He met Byron, whom he liked at once (and whom he delightfully makes fun of in his Journal) and, most gratifying, the Prince Regent. But although he enjoyed London society he could never keep away from Scotland for long. He was quickly back and by the end of the year working on *The Antiquary*, which repeated the success of *Waverley*. At this time the business problems which were to prove so disastrous later were troubling Scott. He had for some time been overreaching himself financially. He was spending vast sums on Abbotsford, on entertaining and helping his friends and on trying to save the business of the Ballantyne brothers. His novels were making money in a way he had never foreseen and this encouraged a false confidence in his financial position.

His first bout of serious illness followed these difficulties. *Rob Roy*, *The Heart of Midlothian* and *The Bride of Lammermoor* were all written during this illness. He was often so ill he could not hold a pen and had to dictate his work. More worrying, he seemed to be suffering a decline in popularity. But this trend was soon reversed with the publication of *Ivanhoe* in 1820. Here was something new. The author of *Waverley* moved out of Scotland and ventured further back in time and further afield than he had done before. He was entering the territory of the Gothic romance and producing something that in its vividness, its grasp of character and its vigour was quite fresh. *Ivanhoe* looked as if it was going to be the most popular of all his novels.

Scott was very deliberate in deciding to move out of the confines of Scotland. He was afraid that if he continued to write only about Scotland he might 'wear out the public favour, unless some mode could be devised to give an appearance of novelty to subsequent productions'. In his introduction to *Ivanhoe* he frankly admits that his attempt to break new ground arose directly from a concern with his public.

With *Ivanhoe* Scott entered on a new phase of writing, and we cease to be able to place his novels so easily in chronological groups. Those that follow sometimes return to Scotland for their subject matter, and sometimes go as far off as Constantinople. But, although it is common to consider that Scott's career as a great novelist ended in 1819 (with perhaps *Redgauntlet*, published in 1824, as a resurrection of his talent), we shall see that such a view ignores some of his very best writing and very best treatments of history. In *Ivanhoe* he created an atmosphere quite different from that of the Scottish novels, inevitably less immediate and more imagined, but in fact it was an attempt to approach the past in very much the same way. Set in the England of Richard the Lionheart, into which he crams historical detail that ranges anachronistically back to 1066, *Ivanhoe* immediately took on some of the colour of romantic medievalism. The details of dress and armour, of tournaments and horses' trappings, yielded more to the imagination than most of the subjects Scott had handled up to now. But to consider that for this reason there should be more emphasis on the romance rather than the historical in our estimation of *Ivanhoe* is very misleading.

There are a number of novels that are generally placed in the same category as *Ivanhoe*—*Quentin Durward*, *The Talisman*, *Kenilworth*, the novels that we are used to seeing in children's editions or transformed into third-rate films. They are novels which at first seem to be pageantry rather than history, fiction built out of romantic plotting rather than from historical feeling. In fact in most cases, in *Quentin Durward* in particular, these novels represent no less serious an attempt on the part of Scott to grapple with the past than *Waverley* or *The Heart of Midlothian*. In all Scott's novels plot comes second to events, and *Ivanhoe* is no exception. The fact that Ivanhoe, the nameless knight, rescues the Jewess Rebecca and marries the Saxon Rowena is less important than the events that surround these activities, even though these events do not have the intrinsic strength that we find in Scott's best novels. Gurth the swineherd, Wamba the jester, the sinister power of the Knights Templar, the grand tournament at Ashby-de-la-Zouche—all these combine to form a background of living without which the King himself and the fight for political power would have no meaning. The joining of hero and heroine does not need this background. The conflict of King and Prince does, and in fact Ivanhoe and Rowena are contributory parts of this background rather than figures set against a pattern of kings and knights that is essentially irrelevant to their fate. If Scott had been writing a historical romance in the tradition already established the latter would have been the case.

Scott had already written novels that were not based on the major historical conflicts that were the parents of the modern age. Neither *Guy Mannering* nor *The Antiquary* were historical novels in this sense. But they were both set in Scotland and dealt with the encroachment of a new society on an old world. The so-called 'historical romances' were set too far back in time to be moulded around this kind of conflict. Their relevance to the contemporary age could not be so directly drawn. The basic antagonisms of Catholic and Protestant, Tory and Whig, which were still so alive in Scott's own day, could not be transplanted indiscriminately. But Scott did find in Richard I's England, or in Louis XI's France in *Quentin Durward*, similar patterns of conflict. The theme of a new society replacing an old reappears in *Ivanhoe*. We see the last vestiges of Saxon England, native simplicity and native breeding, trying to make a final stand against the elaborate power of the Normans—and, ironically, finding as a figurehead Richard himself, who is no less Norman than his perfidious brother Prince John. In *Quentin Durward* there is the conflict of progress and tradition in the personalities and actions of Louis XI, the wily but cautious statesman, and Charles the Bold, the courageous but impetuous feudal lord.

It is a mistake, then, to see the novels that do not fall into the Scottish group as intrinsically less interesting and inferior, just as it is a mistake to see Scott's writing career as falling off from 1820 on. Inevitably when Scott moved into areas that previous novelists had covered, however unsatisfactorily, we are tempted to make comparisons and to hold up for display the features that were obviously borrowed or imitated. We can shake our heads over hidden trap-doors in *Kenilworth*, secret passages in *Woodstock*, and improbable disguise in *The Abbot*, but then we have to admit that the novels themselves survive these. Scott does not introduce secret passages in order to send shivers up and down the spines of his readers. Although he clearly enjoyed some aspects of the Gothic—particularly the kind of modification into

Folk Gothic that we find in, for instance, *The Monastery*—their presence is not of major importance in his novels.

1820 heralded a period of climax in Scott's life. His novels were being published at the rate of two a year. He wrote with confidence, sure that he could produce what his public would enjoy and sure that he could make money. The glorious success of *Ivanhoe* was at first followed by disappointment. *The Monastery*, 1820, did not go down well, and it is certainly one of the most poorly constructed of Scott's novels. But *The Abbot* which came six months later was much more popular. Scott was by this time the leader of cultivated society in Edinburgh. His company was always being sought. He was a man both admired and loved, and a man who did not stint his own admiration and love for others. His life was divided between Castle Street and Abbotsford, between the law and writing, between the gently wild Border hills and the confidently ordered squares and crescents of the New Town. His family were growing up, his elder daughter married to John Gibson Lockhart, who was to become Scott's first biographer. In 1825, before financial ruin burst on him, his elder son Walter was married, an event of immense importance to Scott, for Walter was his heir and his marriage marked the time for his inheritance to be arranged.

THE FINAL PHASE

Long before 1825 Scott had been feeling the effects of financial strain. He had never really recovered from the money he had lost with the Ballantynes, and his continual extravagances in the equipping of Abbotsford and his inability to resist buying land increased the pressure. He could not afford to stop writing, and he could not afford not to write books that would sell. Critics today are prone to dismissing the novels that were written as it became increasingly necessary for Scott to write for money. Scott, however, was sure of his touch, and as long as he was also sure of his ground—which he definitely was not in, for instance, *Count Robert of Paris*—he could produce good work.

The Monastery (written before the crash) *does* show a marked falling off, but it is still packed with redeeming features. The shapelessness which leaves a number of characters high and dry at the novel's end, the ghostly White Lady of Avenel, who is neither fully explained nor allowed to remain completely mysterious, the stilted characterisation of the monks, these we must criticise. The history and the atmosphere of the novel are confused. But the opening, the final battle and many of the incidents are full of power. With authoritative brevity Scott sketches in the background to his own area of Border country as it was in the 16th century, the difficult country dominated by the abbeys and the monasteries on the one hand, and the Border marauders on the other. The opening episode of the flight across the treacherous bog to the lonely tower of Glendearg shows Scott at his best. It is tense and dramatic, yet it is also simple, and the treatment is delicate. But later the novel is marred by unnecessary complications, too many bits and pieces of external influence which confuse Scott's grasp of his subject. The end of the novel recovers, and the plot which had lost itself in second-rate mystery suddenly revives to carry us breathlessly back into history again.

The Abbot carries on the story a generation later. The monastery has been destroyed. Catholicism is virtually outlawed and Mary Queen of Scots is held prisoner. In many ways the political issue here is more clearly focused. It is centred around a major historical figure—Mary, and a major event—her escape from Loch Leven and the Battle of Langside. The anti-climax of Mary's defeat is the anti-climax of history, not of plot, and as usual Scott is at his best when the past governs the plot rather than the plot misusing the past. The construction is tighter, the pace faster and the characterisation has greater depth than in the earlier novel. And the theme is held together by an association of recurring pictures and symbols which counteract some of the novel's cruder moments.

The Abbot and *The Monastery* are both set in pre-1600 Scotland. *The Monastery* at least is not built around a major historical conflict, and it illustrates a tendency that is characteristic of Scott. When he is not handling solid history he comes to rely much more on locality for the novel's strength. In *The Monastery*, locality is forced to provide more than it safely can. It has both to contain and heighten such conflict as there is, and the result is that Scott drags out of it elements of the supernatural and into it foreign colour in the shape of characters, such as Sir Piercie Shafton, who just have no place in the novel's scene. We can see the same thing happening in *The Pirate*, although it is a much better novel than *The Monastery*. Here the mysterious and prophetic Norna of the Fitful Head seems to be forced out of the local atmosphere of the Shetlands and she loses touch with the core of the plot.

This feeling that the characters in *The Pirate* are disjointed and unrelated to what is really going on is reflected in the sister heroines Brenda and Minna. They are presented as opposites in character, and we look for this opposition to be related to the novel's conflicts. But in fact this does not happen and the novel's end exposes the deficiency. Scott's final words on his two heroines are far too neat and easy; he reduces them to the level of his more conventional heroines and cuts them off from their promised significance. This disperses the novel's strength. Scott himself says that he saw 'much in the wild islands of the Orkneys and Zetland, which I judged might be made in the highest degree interesting, should these isles ever become the scene of a narrative of fictitious events', but although his locality has a very haunting quality, and very nearly a tragic quality, the transplantation of plot to place is not sufficiently sustained by either's natural resources.

1821 also saw the publication of *Kenilworth*. The plot is historically thin and perhaps over-dramatic, but the novel as a whole is strangely successful in its atmosphere and characterisation. The whole range of personalities from the rootless Flibertigibbet to Queen Elizabeth herself shows some of Scott's best handling of character. And here each character, as he enters the main weave of plot and atmosphere, has something essential to contribute. Queen Elizabeth was created as a deliberate parallel to Mary in *The Abbot*, and with the same success. In *The Fortunes of Nigel*, which followed *The Pirate* in 1822, Scott presents us with a portrait of James I and VI. Scott never fails with his great men and women, and his great men and women are always historic. His heroes and heroines can never challenge in sheer power of characterisation the kings, the queens, the Claverhouses or the Cromwells, and this seems to be because they are history, while the heroes and heroines can never be more than fiction. In other words, history *helps* Scott's characterisation, while in most writers we would expect the opposite. We would expect historical fact to be a hindrance to the imagination rather than a stimulant.

The Fortunes of Nigel is a delightful novel, and really a Scottish novel in spite of its London setting. Most of the main characters are Scots, including of course James himself, and the novel's theme is concerned with the circumstances and lives of the Scots who followed James to London. Richie Moniplies is one of Scott's most endearing canny, good-hearted, independent but loyal followers. It is not coincidence that he is the closest in character to James VI. Both, unlike Nigel, the disinherited nobleman seeking his family rights, or George Heriot, the sombre jeweller, retain their Scottish accents and their enjoyment of life is completely unrefined. James wavers between caution and impetuosity, between weakness in the hands of his favourites and a sharp eye for deception. He and Richie between them steal the show, in spite of the fact that George Heriot was originally conceived as a male counterpart to Jeanie Deans.

George Heriot's relatively insignificant role, as compared with Jeanie's, is not helped by the fact that Nigel himself is one of Scott's more active heroes. It is not only that he is more involved in the action than many of Scott's heroes are; his role is a historical one in a way that Waverley's or Morton's are not. There were in fact disinherited Scotsmen who came to the Court in London to plead for favours from James, and all kinds of rivalries and jealousies arose between Englishman and Scot. The way in which Nigel gets caught up in Court intrigue is perfectly plausible even if all the details are not. Nigel is not the neutral intruder, but an actor in history who cannot escape from its consequences. The novel still ends in the usual way with a happy marriage and good prospects, but whereas in most of Scott's novels such an ending confirms the hero's separateness from history, in *The Fortunes of Nigel* it does not interfere with the main themes. It is an artificial and conventional means of rounding off events; but, after all, history never stops; fiction has to.

It is neither very easy nor very useful to sort into categories the novels that Scott wrote in the last ten years of his life. While his position in Edinburgh society had never been so secure, his popularity as a writer was not what it was. *Peveril of the Peak* was published in 1823. He had found it hard to write and it was not well received. *Quentin Durward* followed in the same year and was not thought a great deal of in Britain. But on the Continent, where except in Germany little attention had been paid to Scott, it was hugely appreciated. It was the first time Scott had set a novel outside Britain, and he was well rewarded for his pains. Although his picture of France was based on history books and the briefest of visits, the French loved what he had written, and his popularity across the Channel began to rival that of Byron, who was dominating the European imagination.

In fact the French were right to admire *Quentin Durward*, for it contains the most impressive rendering of historical conflict outside the Scottish novels. Quentin, like Nigel, is a historically 'real' figure, and although the fact that he is a Scot uncommitted in French politics makes him to some extent a neutral hero he plays a positive role in the events that involve him. And in this case romance draws him deeper into events rather than becoming a separate section of the plot.

Neither of the two books that 1824 saw published came anywhere near rivalling his old success. *St. Ronan's Well*, the only novel apart from *The Antiquary* in a contemporary setting, did not appeal to a public that relished him as a writer about the past. *Redgauntlet*, his major achievement in so many respects, was received with indifference. But Scott was never discouraged and was always ready to try again—and by this time he *had* to try again. He was always ready to turn to a fresh area of interest and mix a new recipe. The area he turned to in 1825 was that of the crusades, and his 'Tales of the Crusaders', *The Talisman* and

The Betrothed, were published in the same year. These gave him every opportunity for colour and romance, but the moments of excitement do not compensate for the slow pace and the lack of energy in the characterisation.

St. Ronan's Well is more interesting not only because of its handling of contemporary society. It has something of the flavour of *The Bride of Lammermoor*. Clara Mowbray, the tortured heroine, has much in common with Lucy Ashton, although she is a more positive character. She is one of the very few of Scott's heroines who is a victim of circumstances and suffers through the actions and personalities of others. And this being so, one is not surprised at the unhappy ending. Clara Mowbray is far from being a Rose Bradwardine who is so clearly destined for a happy life with the hero. Her independence, her eccentricities which are something like Di Vernon's but without the latter's gaiety and resilience, mark her down for insecurity.

Scott sets his unhappy story amongst the brittle values of a small watering place of growing fashion. Side by side with the changeable eccentricities of Clara and the guilt feelings of Tyrrel, the hero, are the superficialities and malice of this tiny corner of the fashionable world. They are presented uncompromisingly, but not without humour, and this results in a disturbing contrast which Scott is not always able to keep under control. His own attitude is not clear. In some ways he seems to have had a moral purpose in *St. Ronan's Well*, whereas in most of his novels he is concerned with the much larger and more significant framework of ethics. In *The Bride of Lammermoor* the ingredients of tragedy are very precisely worked out. In *St. Ronan's Well* Scott appears to be suggesting that the ironies and contradictions of the standards of society are to blame for Clara's death, but we are never made quite to understand the forces that are at work there.

Scott's public was rather bewildered by a novel that was so different in tone and purpose from what they had come to expect. There is no romance here, few characters whose colour we can enjoy though several at whom we can shudder. Scott himself was not very pleased with the book. It was one thing to create tragedy out of the clash of different ways of life, another to force it into the framework of a still changing contemporary society. But in his next novel, *Redgauntlet*, he was handling a subject that he could readily shape into what became his most impressive statement on Scotland's past.

'REDGAUNTLET'

When it was published, *Redgauntlet* was not seen as the culmination of what Scott had to say about the forces that contributed to contemporary Scotland. But it does in fact draw together Scott's major historical themes, and presents the conflict of the outdated, heroic, romantic past and the progressive, reasoning present on its most fully realised level. In allowing himself two heroes, Alan Fairford and Darsie Latimer, Scott allows himself two lines of approach and a continual dialogue between them. This dialogue, in the form of letters between the unexcitable Alan and the romantically inclined Darsie, builds up a more profound, more sensitive and more comprehensive comment than Scott anywhere else achieves. And in the contrast of personalities and places and the continual movement between reasonable Edinburgh and the dangerous Solway, in the many characters who are links between the old and the new, the known and the unknown, Scott creates his richest social pattern. Although so much of the novel seems to be static, it in fact contains more movement and more action, though not on a grand scale, than we often find in Scott.

Nothing in *Redgauntlet* is on a grand scale, and this is one of the points the novel is making: action on a grand scale belongs to the past. The confrontations in the novel are between personalities, between ways of life and ways of belief, and they are no less significant than the clash of armies. When Redgauntlet himself, the last of the Jacobites, the last to make a stand for the old Cause, is defeated without a sword being drawn, this is the sign of the coming of a new age. It is no paradox that this final scene should be so magnificently and powerfully anti-climactic: it is the very point that Scott is making, and towards which every incident in the novel contributes.

In November 1825 Scott began to keep his Journal, and almost the first thing he had to record was the swiftly approaching financial crisis. By January 1826 the crash had come. Constable's went bankrupt and brought Scott down with it. The Journal reveals the immense strain from which Scott suffered during these months. He forced himself to carry on as usual. From Cockburn we get some idea both of Scott's standing in Edinburgh and the general sympathy with which the disaster was viewed:

> The opening of the year 1826 will ever be sad to those who remember the thunderbolt which then fell on Edinburgh in the utterly unexpected bankruptcy of Scott. . . . If an earthquake had swallowed half the town, it would not have produced greater astonishment, sorrow, and dismay. . . . How humbled we felt when we saw him—the pride of us all, dashed from his lofty and honourable station, and all the fruits of his well-worked talents gone. He had not then even a political enemy. There is not one of those whom his thoughtlessness had so sorely provoked, who would not have given every spare farthing he possessed to retrieve Sir Walter. Well do I remember his first appearance after this calamity was divulged, when he walked into Court one day in January 1826. There was no affectation, and no reality, of *facing it*; no look of indifference or defiance: but the manly and modest air of a gentleman conscious of some folly, but of perfect rectitude, and of most heroic and honourable resolutions.

How difficult it was for Scott to maintain this control we can see from his Journal. Always hopeful that the business would sort itself out, he still managed to survive the shock of each new disaster.

The family had to leave 39 Castle Street although the trustees who took over his affairs allowed him to remain at Abbotsford. When in Edinburgh Scott now stayed in meagre lodgings and lived very plainly. He vowed to give up entertaining on such a lavish scale. He himself was able to sustain the worst that happened and to carry on writing, but it grieved him greatly to see the effect of the disaster on his wife and his daughter Anne, the only child still living with them. His wife was not to survive long. The troubles probably hastened her death, which occurred the following May.

Scott himself had six more years of life in front of him. Although his health was growing steadily worse he was still writing as hard as ever. Almost all the money he now earned from his books went to the trustees to pay off his debts. When the crash came he was in the middle of *Woodstock* and also writing with great gusto his life of Napoleon. From his Journal it is quite clear that he had to force himself to carry on, partly to occupy his mind, partly for the money. It is amazing that *Woodstock* survives so well: it is often singled out by critics as being the highest achievement of his last years.

Woodstock is set in Cromwell's England before Charles II had made his escape. The Royalists, in their defeat, represent a way of life that the Puritans are in the process of destroying. If it is decadent, it is also lively, and though the Cavaliers are portrayed as weak and silly, there is something sinister and at the same time ludicrous about Cromwell's men. (Scott goes much further in his caricature of puritanism than he does in *Old Mortality*.) The hero whose loyalties span the two causes, Markham Everard, has a more important function than we usually find. He follows Cromwell not out of religious fanaticism but from a rational belief in progress. At the same time his close friend Wildrake is a Royalist, a far from sober citizen, and Everard himself is in love with the daughter of an old man who is prepared to give his life for his king. Everard is the necessary link, the necessary mean by which we can judge the two sides. In *Redgauntlet* we have two heroes each with leanings in opposite directions. Everard is both these heroes in one—though his character is not so interesting as his function. He is disgusted by the fanaticism of his comrades and admires the old-fashioned courage of Sir Henry Lee. He is able to see the best and worst of both sides.

Perhaps because of this important balancing function of Everard, *Woodstock*'s rather woolly construction has an appearance of neatness. Scott admits in his Journal that on completing the second volume of the three-volume novel he had no idea how the plot was to be resolved. Perhaps the top-heavy, over-dramatic climax was a result of this. The writing is concentrated, the mood often tense, but the ending topples the plot into shallow melodrama, and the novel is without the ranging depth that we find in Scott at his best. A comparison with *Redgauntlet* immediately reveals its limitations. *Redgauntlet* moves freely over a tiny but significant moment in history. *Woodstock* concentrates on a well-known historic action, Charles II's escape, whose drama is its main feature. Although some of Scott's major conflicts are obviously present in the novel, ultimately it is drama rather than a historical point that these yield.

In 1827 Scott finished his biography of Napoleon and began to write *Tales of a Grandfather* for his little grandson, the Lockhart's eldest child who was to die before Scott himself. In the winter of that year his *Chronicles of the Canongate*, first series, a collection of shorter stories including the very fine *Two Drovers*, was published. These were well received, and briefly restored his popularity to something like what it had been at the time of *Ivanhoe*. All the time he was writing he was fighting with illness and the effects of bankruptcy. He was having to rely on other people, his servants and friends, for he no longer had any family around him. He could not go for a walk without someone to support him, and there were few whom he liked to ask for such support. The horizons of his life were closing in, yet he was still able to produce novels packed with fresh interest.

Certainly the best of his final novels is *The Fair Maid of Perth*, published in the spring of 1828 as the second series of *Chronicles of the Canongate*. Here we have for the first time a novel whose action is dominated by the solid and rising middle class, the burghers of the town of Perth. The most authoritative and active character in the novel is Henry Gow, the courageous yet reasonable blacksmith. Into his description goes a mixture of the noble and courageous, and the old and humble. 'There was daring and resolution in the dark eye, but the other features seemed to express a bashful timidity, mingled with good humour', his forehead 'was high and noble, but the lower part of his face was less happily formed.' We can see in these brief phrases what

Scott was trying to do in his characterisation of Henry Gow: he was trying to present a man who could contain something of the qualities of each level of society. He is partly handsome, partly ugly, courageous, yet full of a sound common sense, capable of passion yet never prevented from quick action by his emotions. Whereas in Jeanie Deans we have a humble character whose simplicity is her strength, in Henry we have a symbol of middle-class power and prosperity who has become this through the touches of a superior nobility in his personality and behaviour.

It is chiefly the personality and function of Henry that give *The Fair Maid of Perth* its strength. Some of the supporting characterisation is less successful, but this is made up for by the novel's two climactic moments—the murder of Prince David and the battle of the clans. The strange spectacle of the two clans destroying each other in front of the King, and the bitter triumph of Henry Gow who joins the battle to take personal vengeance on Conachar, the cowardly Highlander, end the novel on a disturbing note which Henry's marriage and his decision to hang up his sword do not dispel.

Scott's last three novels could not match *The Fair Maid of Perth*. *Count Robert of Paris*, 1830, is probably the least successful product of his career. His lack of grasp of his subject, his lack of intimacy with his characters, are only too apparent. *Anne of Geierstein*, which came the year before, is more interesting, although it was written under no more propitious circumstances. Scott was conscious that *Count Robert* was going badly, but *Anne of Geierstein* he wrote quickly without reference books to check his historical background and with little idea of where the novel was taking him. The final third or so shows signs of this; we are conscious of the machinery creaking in the attempt to bring the plot to some sort of conclusion. But the earlier part set in the newly independent cantons of Switzerland moves at a fast and sure pace. It is amazing that Scott was able to capture so convincingly the tenor of life in a country he had never visited at a period that he was remembering from the history books of his youth.

Scott's last novel, *Castle Dangerous*, was published in 1831, but even in the final months of his life he had plans for another. In 1831, too, he went on his last trip abroad which took him to Italy and the Mediterranean. He was really too ill to gain very much from it. On his return he had to make a prolonged stay in London to recover strength for the last leg of his journey. It was widely known that he was ill, and the whole of London seemed to be waiting anxiously for news of his health. But he was in fact in a coma most of the time and not able to enjoy these signs of appreciation. In July of 1832 he was able to continue his journey home to Abbotsford. He lived for another two months, completely unable to write and most of the time in a state of half-consciousness.

Scott died in the year of the first Reform Bill, a year that seemed to herald the Victorian era. His death marked the end of what had been one of Scotland's culturally most lively and distinctive periods. We cannot imagine Scott surviving into the Victorian age, or tackling history in terms of Victorian society. He was very much a novelist of change, of a period of history when it was just as possible to look back to the old ways as forward to the new. But even though we cannot place him in the society and events of the later 19th century his influence was immense. It is on the continent that we can see this influence most clearly at work—on Balzac and Victor Hugo in France, on Manzoni in Italy, on Tolstoy in Russia, to mention only a few. In Britain, literature lost touch with Scott much more quickly (though we find continual reference to his novels in, for instance, the Brontës and Mrs. Gaskell), and while in France and Germany he is still revered, here he is little read and has little critical attention paid to him.

SCOTT'S HUMANITY

It is easiest to approach Scott simply through his humanity, through his wonderfully sympathetic and balanced grasp of character, through his widely sweeping yet detailed understanding of the extremes and contrasts of life. He loved men, yet could not excuse the savage society men had made. It was his humanity that made him an optimist and a romantic. Although he did not turn a blind eye to the worst, he could always see the best, and he always had faith in human nature. Scott's themes are themes of conflict because he himself was torn between two ways of life and two visions of what life ought to be. In this he was like his heroes, but unlike his heroes he was too deeply involved to be able to extract himself from the consequences of history. And this helped to resolve what would have been yet another contradiction: he was involved, he was committed, yet he was balanced.

In the following chapters we will discuss in greater detail particular aspects of Scott's fiction. We will try to balance the common criticisms of his writing against his clearly recognisable triumphs and his more elusive partial successes. The usual assessment of Scott is that he was a commanding but greatly flawed novelist who perhaps produced one 'great' novel—*The Heart of Midlothian*. Scott was not a great stylist, but we will try to show that he was a great creator of character and atmosphere, a great recorder of social detail, and above all revolutionary in his fictional handling of history—and that, in this role, his most outstanding work is *Redgauntlet*.

5

Plot and Construction in the Waverley Novels

At the time Scott was writing, the accepted length for a novel was a great deal longer than it is now. This simple fact accounts for some of the features of Scott's plots and construction. From the start Scott knew that he had plenty of space, that he need be in no hurry, that there was time for a large range of characters and events. In most of the novels of the 18th and 19th centuries we do not look for tightness and economy of construction. When we find it it is usually in novels where space and locality are deliberately confined and given set bounds—in the novels of Jane Austen, for instance. Here the fact that most of her characters move only within the boundaries of one or two houses and their grounds and immediate surroundings influences the structure of the novels. Although Jane Austen's writing is always relaxed, her plots are more tensely held together than anything we find in Scott. Her characters progress and her points are made by careful development rather than by the kind of successive illustration we find in Fielding or Smollett.

The latter novelists allow their characters complete freedom of movement. Incident follows incident without there being a particular central point. The incidents are often repetitive, and illustrate the same facets of the hero's character; but if this is done with sufficient comedy—as it is in *Tom Jones*—then this does not worry us. There is a whole series of climaxes and anti-climaxes and the novel could go on for ever. The author simply has to select a suitable moment for leaving his hero adequately set up. He can then be left and the novel can end.

It may at first seem that this is how Scott too constructs his plots. There is something arbitrary and lax about the way his novels are put together. Characters are sometimes hastily disposed of at the novel's end as if Scott just did not know what to do with them when the time came for him to round off his plot. His long introductory beginnings are often hard to get through and there are frequent lapses and divergencies in the middle which seem to interrupt the main movement. But before approaching the question of Scott's plotting and structure it is important to remember what is perhaps a very obvious but yet a crucial fact: Scott was virtually the first novelist to write about real people and real events of the past. The only comparable writer in this respect was Shakespeare, and his treatment of history was entirely different. The fact that Scott was writing historical novels that involved a great deal more than simply setting his plots in the past underlies the structure of all his novels.

THE INFLUENCE OF HISTORY

Scott begins with a particular historical period; the time of the first Jacobite rebellion, for instance. His period is defined not only by what happened and who was involved, but by how people lived at that time. And so, in *Rob Roy*, the long approach to the novel's main event is packed with details of what people ate, what they wore, the houses in which they lived, the weapons with which they fought. Scott's love of this kind of detail is apparent as soon as we open one of his novels. Its significance lies in the fact that Scott is writing about something of almost greater importance—some would not qualify this—than history's large events: he is writing about society. He is writing about society in a way that is very different from Fielding's or Richardson's or Jane Austen's approach. These three novelists write about manners and morals. Jane Austen takes a minute slice of society and examines it in detail. Fielding and Richardson range more widely. But Scott is not concerned with making moral judgments, and when he does write about manners—in *Guy Mannering* or *St. Ronan's Well*—he does not lose touch with the larger social framework and the smaller social details of the kind mentioned above.

We always have to bear in mind Scott's history when we are discussing his plots. It can be said that Scott is describing historical events and personalities in a fictional setting, or that he is placing a fictional plot in an environment of historical reality. The important point is that there are two forces at work which Scott has to bring under control. He has to control and give shape to historical fact so that it makes fictional sense, and he has to mould his characters and their actions so that they are not at odds with history, and can be clearly seen as products of the society Scott is portraying.

Above all, Scott has to be convincing. This is the object of the necessary control. He has to convince us that the result of his bringing his imagination and understanding to bear on historical events is real. It is less important that we accept Edward Waverley than it is that we believe in the Jacobite Rebellion as Scott presents it. It does not matter if we find Frank Osbaldistone a little feeble, if we are convinced of the truth of the way of life and attitudes of characters like Nicol Jarvie and Rob Roy himself. And, creating the kinds of heroes that he does, Scott is aware of this. It is for this reason that Scott begins with history rather than with his plot. It is this that explains why, although he so often admitted that when he began a novel he had no idea how it would end, he was still able to produce controlled and meaningful fiction. Scott did not have to invent military victories and defeats or political clashes, or the actions of great figures in history. His imagination did not have to furnish Cromwells and Claverhouses. The action and the drama and the great men were all there. Scott had to make them convincing by giving them meaning and purpose in terms of his fiction. But he did not have to bring them to a close. In fact, he *could* not bring them to a close. When he settles his heroes and heroines happily, and neatly disposes of his other characters, he is simply putting a conventionally artificial full-stop in mid-historical sentence.

Scott *does* convince because his writing grows out of period and locality. Even when we begin with the intruder, with

Waverley or Quentin Durward or Frank Osbaldistone, this contains something significant about the time and place. The fact that Waverley is completely innocent about Jacobitism is a reflection on the Rebellion itself as well as a reflection of Waverley's character. The fact that Quentin is an exiled Scot seeking his fortune in France is an important historical point as well as a major factor in the novel's plotting. This is our first clue to the construction of the Waverley novels. The basic features of the plot are historical. They are produced by the society Scott describes. But, as we shall see, quite frequently many of the details and the incidents, and a few of the characters, are historically neutral and unnecessary, and it is when we come to these that we begin to worry about how Scott put his novels together.

Although the conventional endings suggest this, there is usually no real separation between plot and history, in spite of moments of divergence. The mysterious White Lady in *The Monastery* is an example of a factor that is forced to be essential to the plot but which is at odds with the novel's history. Her presence is annoying because Scott does not make his own attitude to her clear. It is perhaps unfair to choose a 'spirit' as an example of a floating character, but Sir Piercie Shafton in the same novel is another. They are both serious flaws since it is, above all, character that binds plot and history. The neutral hero, for instance, is almost always provided with a companion whose roots are in the social realities of the time. Cuddie Headrigg gives Henry Morton an intimate link with the more everyday realities and expediencies of his commitment. *Waverley*'s Callum Beg faces Edward with some of the grimmer facts of clan warfare. It is through characters like these, as well as through his contact with great historical figures, that the peripheral activities of the hero—the romantic aspects of the plot—are brought firmly within the sphere of historical fact.

POINTS OF CONTACT

Wherever we look we are faced with massed points of contact of this kind. These are links across time and across social barriers.

Most important, they are links between old and new ways of life, for it is, above all, ordinary people who are most harshly exposed to the changing times. Scott does not neglect this level of historical continuity. In *Guy Mannering* it is Meg Merrilies who provides the clue to Bertram's past. She, the last of her race in that locality, brings together father and son. She has suffered at the hands of the father and devotes herself to bringing justice to the son. She has paved the way for a new generation. The significance here is twofold. Bertram is helpless without the assistance of people whose station in life has brought them into contact with the harshest processes of history. (Bertram has been hard done by, but he retains all the qualities of his class, which allow him to slip into his allotted place as a gentleman when the time comes.) And Meg knows more about Bertram than anyone else because she has never lived at a distance from the crueller realities of life.

Scott is putting his novels together from a much wider range of experience than any novelist before him, and he is trying all the time to tie these different kinds of experience together. He does not do this by arranging a giant climax in which all his characters are involved. He does it much more historically by illustrating the waves of influence that people and events set in motion. The Porteous Riots in *The Heart of Midlothian* are a good example. It is this incident more than anything else that brings together Jeanie Deans and the Duke of Argyle. At the same time, Jeanie herself is a link between Edinburgh and London and between the common people and the Court. The structure of contact in Scott's novels can be very complex, but we are rarely so much aware of the complexities that we are distracted from their point.

This kind of structure does allow Scott great flexibility, and it is the way Scott uses this flexibility with complete freedom that some critics who look continually for tight patterns of meaning find unacceptable. But it is Scott's flexibility in his handling of plot and history which allows him to devote so much time to characterisation and to particular incidents that allow his characters to show their paces at the same time as being historically authentic. It is this flexibility that allows him so much comedy, and prevents the comedy from challenging the history: so that the comment of Alick Polworth, when he and Waverley are leaving Carlisle after the execution of Fergus MacIvor and Evan Dhu, is as appropriate as a more sombre reflection: 'The heads are ower the Scotch yate, as they ca' it. It's a great pity of Evan Dhu, who was a very well-meaning, good-natured man, to be a Hielandman; and indeed so was the Laird o' Glennaquoich too, for that matter, when he wasna in ane o' his tirrivies.' There are hundreds of examples in the Waverley novels of moments when the serious and the dramatic melt into the comic with complete propriety: Cuddie Headrigg at the trial, for example, or the description of the unhappy fate of the Laird of Balmawhapple which makes the final word on the Battle of Prestonpans in *Waverley* a comic one.

It is difficult to find a novelist with whom we can compare Scott in this respect. There is perhaps only Dickens, yet the fact that his purpose was almost always contemporary made his task that much easier. Scott managed comedy without losing his grip on history, and this too has to be taken into consideration in a discussion of plot and construction. The conflicts which are at the root of the Waverley novels' action are an ideal breeding ground for comic as well as serious clashes, and the fact that both can grow from the same seed is yet another source of comedy. The kind of extremism that Scott so frequently handles invites comic treatment. Extremism has bred the passionate dignity of Redgauntlet; it has also bred the comic types who are obsessive on a less serious level.

Only on one or two occasions—the puritans in *Woodstock* are an example—does Scott allow his comic characters to be cut off from the main movement of plot and theme. The currents of reaction between the comic and the serious are almost always switched on. The novels have to allow space and time for these currents to flow between all their various elements. Scott could of course have told his stories much more quickly and economically. But if we cut his novels down to the bare bones of their plots (if, in other words, we insist that there is nothing to fiction but plot) what have we left? We have got rid of almost everything that makes Scott's novels what they are.

SCOTT'S MATERIAL

The fact that Scott deals with major political events and personalities inevitably leads to a certain shapelessness. He could not wilfully impose a shape on history that history could not take. He builds his novels' form out of other factors, which are also an essential part of history—out of locality, out of character and out of the natural drama of historical conflict. A novel in which there is no major event yet which is important for its history is *Rob Roy*. We can see the effect of this. Scott charts various strands of Jacobite revolt—the Tory gentry of the North of England, the Catholic priests, the Highland outlaws—and tests the climate of the period as he goes. But it is a slow process, for there are no major historical figures—excepting Rob Roy himself, to whom we are introduced so ambiguously—and no large events to bring the situation dramatically into focus. The issues are large, however; but it is not until we meet Baillie Nicol Jarvie whose particular brand of local lucidity does so much to put the plot into gear that we begin to understand what the issues really are.

The structure of *Rob Roy* is curiously lop-sided. Frank Osbaldistone's long malingering at Osbaldistone Hall while the skeleton of the mystery is rather jerkily put together is only just saved from being tedious by the vivacity of Di Vernon and the superb villainy of her cousin Rashleigh. Scott waits until he has assembled all the machinery of his plot before he gives it free rein. Then, with the help of Andrew Fairservice and the Baillie, the pace, the comedy and the significance quicken as the Lowlanders make their cautious way into Highland territory. It is almost as if Scott is deliberately holding back our understanding so that it matches the slowly dawning awareness of Frank himself.

STRUCTURE AND HISTORICAL CONFLICT: 'OLD MORTALITY'

We can see Scott's structure at its best in the novels where the major historical conflicts are immediately established, although

Waverley, where this is not the case, is admirably clear and controlled in its construction. In a late novel, *Anne of Geierstein*, the structure of the greater part of the novel depends almost completely on historical confrontation and when, near the end, the plot begins to lapse, it is because the historical conflicts have petered out and Scott is merely trying to keep his characters occupied.

Old Mortality shows Scott's control of plot and construction at something near its best. (*Redgauntlet* is the novel in which one can find least to criticise.) The historical conflict here is interestingly handled, for the two sides, Royalist and Covenanter, are represented differently. We see the Royalists almost entirely through and in the personality of Claverhouse. He is a completely dominating character. Burley, on the other side, does not wholly bear the burden of acting as Claverhouse's symbolic rival. The forces that oppose Claverhouse are much more intricately represented. We are shown them as products of a way of life, of society, of history in fact. Into Claverhouse is packed all the power of a symbol, and he can contain this with ease because he is so superbly characterised. The opposition to his authority is composed of a wide variety of elements which are illustrated in terms of characters as wide apart as Cuddie Headrigg and Burley.

The climax of this conflict comes with the Battle of Bothwell Brig, about three-quarters of the way through the novel. But although Claverhouse's victory is the climax of action the whole meaning of the event cannot be contained by it. In *Waverley* the Battle of Culloden, which we are accustomed to think of as the climactic event of the '45, is hardly mentioned. What Scott gives us is a picture of the aftermath of the battle. His focus on history is adjusted through the executions at Carlisle rather than through the fact of the Jacobite defeat on Culloden Moor. Similarly, though Scott's description of Bothwell Brig is marvellously done—as are almost all his battle scenes—he does not use it as a symbolic figurehead of history. In other words, he does not use it in the way we tend to learn history at school, pretending that history is composed of climactic events that occurred on certain dates. It is the battle's aftermath that is important, the effect on both the committed and those who were involved in it whether they liked it or not. Scott is concerned with what victory and defeat meant in terms of society and progress.

Of course, Scott enjoyed immensely his descriptions of action on a large scale, and they show a clear grasp of military strategy and tactics as well as an energetic imagination. But it is not description simply for its own sake. Morton's encounter with Claverhouse before the battle (there is no direct confrontation between Claverhouse and the leaders of the Covenanters; their only contact is through Morton), his organisation of the troops under his command, his shocked reaction to the confusion of the rest of the Covenanting army, and the way in which the rebels move into battle all have a much wider importance than the straightforward function of setting the scene for battle. Morton has been Claverhouse's prisoner, but on this occasion he meets him as an equal, although an enemy. They are two gentlemen with a proper sense of military honour, and the meeting reminds us of the great difference between Morton and his fellow insurgents. Morton is not a Burley, ruled by passionate conviction, he is not a religious zealot like Ephraim Macbriar or Habakkuk Mucklewrath. He is a well-bred moderate, and as such it is clear that he is going to be saved from the consequences of extremism.

He places his troops in accordance with his understanding of the military situation, not as dictated by the beliefs for which he is fighting. He fights as if the battle itself means more than the issues that are being contested, and there is a sharp contrast between this and the confusions and jealousies that disorganise his own side. The battle confirms the fact that Morton is no Covenanter, although as a soldier he does perhaps more than any other for them. Scott never shows us the process of a reasonable and moderate man becoming wholly committed in a violent cause. His heroes fight out of a gentlemanly loyalty that is itself the result of a gentlemanly sympathy. They do not really act out of a sense of right and wrong—they do not make moral decisions. They are never in the position of having to weigh up the factors on either side and making a free choice between them. Yet they do, almost always, fight on the *losing* side, and this is very significant, both as a reflection of Scott's idea of a gentleman and on his way of commenting on history.

SCOTT'S CLIMAXES

The Battle of Bothwell Brig is described in such a way as to guide Scott's hero through a historic event and to use him as a pivot for picturing the part played by each side. Henry Morton is the mean against which the other characters are measured. At the same time Morton is continually being measured against the other characters, and the whole novel is constructed so as to show this dual measurement. Bothwell Brig is the novel's historical climax. But the ranging nature of Scott's plotting means that he is in fact managing all kinds of different climaxes right through the novel. At his best Scott keeps a continual sense of movement and a continual sense of the imminent clash or separation of character. In *Old Mortality* this breaks down in the final pages when Morton is brought back to Scotland to tie up the romantic ends—though even this has its meaningful moments, for instance his visit to Cuddie's cottage. But up to the time of his exile the flux of time, space and character energetically spark off new phases of action.

Scott uses his climaxes to draw together his characters, different ways of life, different attitudes and different interests. Frequently he begins his novels with what can only be called a climactic event, even though at first we cannot see its full significance. He does this in *The Heart of Midlothian*, and on a much smaller scale in *Anne of Geierstein*. In *Quentin Durward* it is scaled down still further and becomes a significant encounter. In *Old Mortality* he presents his opening climax in holiday clothing. The wappenschaw gives him the opportunity to provide a portrait of a countryside, its people and its traditions. He covers a wide spectrum of society spiced with sharp little encounters, and the detail of dress and behaviour is there as part of the general colour as well as of particular social observation. The contest itself is an ancient tradition, a tradition that is pointless in terms of the realities of battle yet socially of immense importance. It belongs to the past yet points to the future, for competing in it are three of the novel's most important characters—Morton himself, in partial disguise, Cuddie Headrigg, and Lord Evandale, Morton's romantic rival—and we are shown them first in competition with each other. We see them first in action, but it is action of a particular kind. There is a real sense of rivalry, but the setting is festive. The competitors take their shooting seriously, but the winner is only a holiday hero. The spectators are enjoying themselves, but surrounding them are signs of a much more serious warfare.

Morton's celebration of his victory leads us directly to the presence of Claverhouse's dragoons, his meeting with Burley and the quarrel with Bothwell, the dragoons' sergeant. We begin to see now in what direction the wappenschaw was pointing. Morton has defeated Evandale, aristocrat and Royalist. He is accepted by the ordinary people who frequent the inn as the hero of the day. Yet he is also something of an outcast from polite society: in other words, his social position will not precisely dictate his reaction to any situation. In the inn after the contest Morton intervenes to ensure fair play between Bothwell and Burley, but in doing so he is defying the King's army. The fact that Burley asks for his company and protection as they leave the inn again suggests that Morton has chosen, or that his sense of justice has chosen, the anti-establishment side in a conflict that has not yet matured and in which up to that point he has had no particular interest. We now move on to a different level of conflict—from formal competition to tavern brawl to the novel's crucial struggle between Burley's commitment and Morton's sense of fair play. And soon Scott confronts us with a third element—Claverhouse's authority.

STRUCTURE AND RHYTHM

This is the kind of rhythm that we find in *Old Mortality* and in most of Scott's novels. There is no formal pattern but a flux of congregation and separation. The way the novel develops depends on what characters are brought together at which point. And this is why Scott is able to write as he does, without planning and often without knowing how he is going to wind up the plot. Almost any of the Waverley novels will show how the movement is determined by the meaningful meeting of characters, and these meetings usually contain an element of conflict or else the source of a conflict's resolution. Sometimes these meetings seem to be too coincidental, but in fact, although it can be argued that Scott at times allows coincidence to save his hero or ensure his romantic happiness, it can never be said that he forces *historic* significance out of them.

In *Old Mortality* each climax—the battles, the confrontations between rivals of all kinds—contains elements of resolution and also introduces new aspects of conflict. The wappenschaw establishes Morton simultaneously as victor and outcast and points the way to more serious kinds of competition. The Battle of Bothwell Brig means defeat for the Covenanters—the end of their cause, for the time being, but the beginning of Morton's readjustment to the position of moderate. This is how Scott binds together plot and history. The trial is the next meeting point. Morton is stabilised, as it were, by his growing admiration and understanding of Claverhouse, but his return to level ground is surrounded by the grim and the comic. Macbriar and his fellow fanatics must die. Cuddie, the honest rogue, is pardoned. Morton himself is exiled: as a modern gentleman whose ethos is really the same as that of those who try him he does not have to die but must recognise that he has to pay some price for rebellion.

And so we are left, not with the large facts of victory and defeat but with hints of much more basic and lasting social and political differences. Morton himself is back on the middle road, but he still has two rivals—Burley and Evandale. The first has to be eliminated not only because of his extremism but because Morton has to purge himself of his influence. The second is Morton's rival in love. The fact that Morton has experienced extremism, survived the rigours of battle and punishment and remained undamaged in his personality makes it quite clear that, in Scott's view, he has some kind of natural superiority that will bring him to success in love also. And this is perhaps the point about Scott's heroes. The reasonable man who survives commitment has qualities which, although they may be dull in comparison with past ideas of heroic behaviour, are much more relevant and useful to the modern age with which men like Scott were trying to come to terms.

The moments when Scott's construction seriously lapses are usually the moments when plot and history part company. The winding up of the romantic plot in *Old Mortality* is an example. The marriage of Edward and Rose in *Waverley* is not: Edward's rejection of Flora and choosing of Rose is an important illustration of his function as hero. We tend to think of structure in terms of pace. In *Rob Roy*, it is true, the two are intimately related. But it would be a mistake to condemn as a flaw in structure each time that Scott slows the plot down. *Redgauntlet*'s beginning moves as slowly as *Rob Roy*'s, yet the novel needs precisely this slow, measured development. Scott is more likely to err when he suddenly speeds up the proceedings, as in the end of *The Pirate*, for he *needs* plenty of time and plenty of room to do himself justice.

Scott was writing at a time when theories of fiction had hardly been voiced. These were born of later developments in the novel, but critics are prone to apply them to Scott's writing. We should not look for patterns in Scott's novels, or judge them schematically. It is rhythm that is behind Scott's structure, and we can only follow this rhythm if we approach the Waverley novels without the yardsticks that were provided later.

6

Scott's Style and Characterisation

We do not go to Scott for the subtle pleasures of a careful style, like Jane Austen's, nor for the virtuosity which we find in Dickens or D. H. Lawrence. Scott's style at its worst combines the formality of the 18th century with the sentimentality and prudery of the Victorians, and he is not easily forgiven for it. At its best, it is very readable, once we are used to the slow pace, but not very distinguished. 'Workmanlike' is the adjective which springs to mind, and it is not an epithet which Scott himself would have shunned.

But this tepid judgment must at once be qualified. Wherever Scott sets a man or a woman talking, especially if the speaker is a lower-class character or a Scotsman of any degree, his prose is likely to touch the heights. Each of his best characters speaks prose with its own individual rhythm and life, so that we cannot discuss the prose without talking about the character. It is often objected that the Scottish speech is hard for a modern English reader to understand. It is basically no harder than Shakespeare's prose, and it is often as rewarding. The best approach to it is not to flee to the glossary every time an odd word crops up, but to read it as quickly as possible; one soon finds that words like 'breeks' and 'fou' have become as familiar as 'trousers' and 'drunk'.

Scott's 'own' style, it may be said, is the rather drab wall which sets off his lively portraits. Or perhaps we should compare it to a heavily framed but serviceable window, for Scott's visual imagination and his powers of social observation are easily discerned through it. Often, on going back to examine a passage which seemed to provide inspired writing well above Scott's usual level, we find that the prose is the same heavy prose we expect from him; what made it seem great was the picture which it conjured up or the understanding which flashed through it.

Clumsiness is easily found, and bad grammar is not unknown. Scott wrote very fast and sent his novels quickly through the presses. Even if he had had the temperament of a fastidious stylist, he had no time to be one.

His ponderous euphemisms can be annoying or funny, depending on the reader's patience—as when he refers to the eunuchs in Saladin's court as 'those unhappy officials whom eastern jealousy places round the zenana'. Scott is particularly prone to call a spade 'a traditional agricultural implement of the region' in any case where sex is concerned. When Henry Gow, the blacksmith, leads a 'glee-woman' through the streets of Perth, Scott's attempt to explain his embarrassment reads as follows:

> Ere our stout son of Vulcan had fixed his worship on the Fair Maid of Perth, a certain natural wildness of disposition had placed him under the influence of Venus, as well as that of Mars: and it was only the effect of a sincere attachment which had withdrawn him entirely from such licentious pleasures. Ch. 12

This, alas, is on a par with the pompous 19th-century provincial journalism which Dickens loved to make fun of; and it could be paralleled in any of the novels.

RHYTHM AND LANGUAGE

A fairer example of Scott's 'workmanship' would be this, from *Woodstock*:

> It was often noised about, that Cromwell, the deep and sagacious statesman, the calm and intrepid commander, he who had overcome such difficulties, and ascended to such heights, that he seemed already to bestride the land which he had conquered, had, like many other men of great genius, a constitutional taint of melancholy, which sometimes displayed itself both in words and actions, and had been first observed in that sudden and striking change, when, abandoning entirely the dissolute freaks of his youth, he embraced a very strict course of religious observances, which, upon some occasions, he seemed to consider as bringing him into more near and close contact with the spiritual world. Ch. 9

Is this good prose or bad? Saving the clumsiness of 'as bringing him into', it seems to be neither. The long sentence is typical of Scott, though this is an extreme example. It is slow, and the heavy punctuation (which was usual at the time) slows it down still further; yet it is well-managed. We absorb all the information which it gives without difficulty, and there is a lot of it, nothing less than a brief biography of Cromwell.

The colourless adjectives and the abstract nouns help to sketch the man economically. Words like 'sagacious', 'intrepid', 'genius', 'melancholy', 'dissolute', 'observances' have no 'smell' to them, no life in themselves. But they have the necessary dignity. Their meanings, while they are broad, are quite clear. If we substituted more lively ones—'clever' for 'sagacious', 'moodiness' for 'melancholy', we would immediately be leaving something out or distorting the picture. 'Clever' has pejorative undertones, and it lacks the extra meaning of 'wise' and 'statesmanlike' which 'sagacious' carries. In the same way, the word 'dissolute' covers several types of bad behaviour in one word. Scott's apparently cumbersome Latinisms, in fact, work like a shorthand. They rapidly give us an accurate general impression.

The same efficiency appears in the swifter passages where Scott is describing action. The language is always unobtrusive and predictable. Scott almost never surprises us with his choice of words, and is never sensational in his descriptions of war and danger. Take this moment of suspense in *Waverley*, just as the Battle of Prestonpans is beginning and the hero is about to fight for the first time:

> The clansmen on every side stript their plaids, prepared their arms, and there was an awful pause of about three minutes, during which the men, pulling off their bonnets, raised their faces to heaven, and uttered a short prayer; then pulled their bonnets over their brows and began to move forward at first slowly. Waverley felt his heart at that time throb as it would have burst from his bosom. It was not fear, it was not ardour,—it was a compound of both, a new and deeply energetic impulse, that with its first emotion chilled and astounded, then fevered and maddened his mind. The sounds around him combined to exalt his enthusiasm; the pipes played,

and the clans rushed forward, each in its own dark column. As they advanced they mended their pace, and the muttering sounds of the men to each other began to swell into a wild cry.

Ch. 47

The syntax of this passage is, of course, far looser; the phrases huddle on top of each other, as the actions follow together or in quick succession. There is something very appropriate to the moment in the grammatical oddness of the first sentence; the rhythms of Scott's prose are rarely as subtle as this. But this is not 'fine' writing. There is not one word which gives us pause, or which makes us think, 'how clever of Scott'. This is a virtue; we have nothing to lose by reading fast. Again, we notice the usefulness of Scott's Latinised vocabulary. '. . . ardour . . . energetic impulse . . . enthusiasm' . . . these words stand for typical emotions, not unusual ones, and we hurry over them quickly, with complete comprehension. The Anglo-Saxon words—fear, dark, muttering, wild—are equally plain, equally broad, and equally effective.

Two of Scott's commonest mannerisms emerge from the passages just quoted. 'It was not fear, it was not ardour' shows a habit of mind characteristic of Scott when he is analysing a man's appearance or his feelings or his character. He rejects one or more of the obvious and expected words or phrases in this way, then combines them or plumps for the one which is right. To take a simple comparison, here is Prior Aymer in *Ivanhoe*: 'In his seat he had nothing of the awkwardness of the convent, but displayed the easy and habitual grace of a well-trained horseman.' Scott, dealing with a man, is always concerned to point out whether he is or is not typical, and if so, of what. Waverley might have been expected to feel either fearful or ardent, but in fact felt both. The Prior, instead of representing the *type* of the clumsy monk, conforms to the *type* of the well-trained horseman. Because he is a monk, this at once makes him a moderately complex character instead of a simple one. This obviously goes along with the generalising nature of Scott's vocabulary.

SCOTT'S TENTATIVENESS

A second trait of Scott's writing—a more puzzling one—is illustrated by the word 'seems' near the end of the passage about Cromwell. A novelist, surely, knows all about the characters he chooses to introduce? Two further examples, small matters in themselves, come one after the other in *The Heart of Midlothian*. We are told that Reuben Butler was orphaned '*about* the year 1704–5'. About a page later, we read that old Dumbiedikes used '*pretty nearly* the following words'.

Partly, this must be a habit, a bad one perhaps, of which Scott is unconscious. But we can see how it arose. In the case of Cromwell, he is writing about a real person and going by what his contemporaries said about him. This is the method of the historian, which Scott was bound to follow with his major historical figures. What is odd is that Scott should write in the same way about purely fictitious personages. Two important points emerge. The first is that Scott was thinking of his novels as 'true' history, and adopting the caution of a scholar. The second is that he sees his invented people from the outside, as their friends or even a casual observer might have seen them, rather than from the inside, like a modern 'psychological' novelist. When he does get 'inside' Edward Waverley, he uses generalised language, so that the character is typical rather than sharply individual.

Scott's prose is mainly impersonal; except when it is bad we usually forget about it, and so forget about its author. (One could never say this of Dickens, or Graham Greene, who constantly take us aback with their personal and surprising use of language.) But he carries on from the 18th century the tradition of the author's comment. He quite often steps in to remind us that the people he is describing, though born long ago, have their counterparts in the present day; that is, he moralises about his characters. (See, for instance, the beginning of Chapter 22 of *Kenilworth*, where he makes Amy Robsart's interest in clothes the excuse for poking ponderous fun at 'ladies of fashion of the present or any other period'.) He is never afraid to tell the reader why he has left something out, or to remind him of the situation of characters who have been out of sight for a while. How well 'our reader' takes this kind of thing depends on how much he likes Scott's personality and how many of Scott's elephantine witticisms he can stomach. But, like Scott's caution which has just been discussed, these 'asides' sometimes have the effect of reminding us that we are reading not what the author *chooses* to tell us, but what he *can* tell us. Scott is ready to remind us of the limits of his own knowledge of people and periods, or to apologise for the sometimes clumsy results of that free-wheeling narrative method which we have analysed.

In fact, he produces something like the famous 'alienation-effect' in Bertolt Brecht's plays, and for similar reasons. Just as Brecht wishes to prevent the audience from sympathising with his stage characters as if they were real people, so Scott is candidly anxious to instruct and entertain the reader, but not to lead him astray. The historical detail he will vouch for as fairly accurate (often directly, in a footnote), but the mechanics of his plot, which he hopes will amuse the reader, are not to be taken seriously.

LANDSCAPE

In the same way, his descriptions of landscape are not so much self-conscious as reader-conscious. When he pauses to describe a scene, he will usually take one of two attitudes; that of the practical farmer, or that of the gentleman of taste. The polished Georgian traveller had learnt to admire 'the picturesque', and was willing to sally out to sketch a 'wild' scene if it was not too far from civilised creature-comforts. In some novels—*Guy Mannering*, for instance, or *The Pirate*—Scott gives us the raw 'feel' of desolate country. But even in the latter novel, where the ruggedness of the Shetlands is strongly evoked, Scott steps in to remind us at one point that only a particular type of weather produces:

> that variety of light and shade which often gives to a bare and unenclosed scene, for the time at least, a species of charm approaching to the varieties of a cultivated and planted country. Ch. 7

Scott will find a mountain 'sublime' or a view 'grand', but he knows that the grandeur of the Highlands goes along with the poverty of their inhabitants. When Jeanie Deans sees the fertile, well-populated country round the Thames for the first time on her way to Windsor, Scott steps in to call the scenery 'unrivalled'. So it is—in terms of the prosperity it brings to the farmers and the comfort of its inhabitants. Scott sympathises with Jeanie's reaction to this 'luxuriance', of course:

> 'It's braw rich feeding here for the cows, and they have a fine breed o' cattle here . . . but I like just as weel to look at the craigs of Arthur's seat, and the sea coming in ayont them, as at a' thae muckle trees.'
> Ch. 36

For this is the reaction of the patriotic Scotsman or woman, especially of one who has only known her own country until the last few days. As a practical farmer Jeanie is envious.

Gentlemen of the period, however, were connoisseurs of scenes as well as of paintings. They had rules for appraising both. When Scott, in *The Monastery*, describes his own Border country, we find him appraising it for them.

> The mountains, as they would have been called in England, *Scotticé* the steep *braes*, rose abruptly over the little glen, here presenting the grey face of a rock, from which the turf had been peeled by the torrents, and there displaying patches of wood and copse, which had escaped the waste of the cattle and the sheep of the feuars, and which, feathering naturally up the beds of empty torrents, or occupying the concave recesses of the bank, gave at once beauty and variety to the landscape. Above these scattered woods rose the hill in barren, but purple majesty; the dark rich hue, particularly in autumn, contrasting beautifully with the thickets of oak and birch, the mountain ashes and thorns, the alders and quivering aspens, which chequered and varied the descent, and not less with the dark green and velvet turf, which composed the level part of the narrow glen.

The language is interesting. Nature 'displays' and 'presents' her charms as a painter shows off his skills. 'Contrast' and 'variety' are looked for in a landscape. Could woods 'feather' *un*naturally? Yes, because it was then the job of a landscape gardener to provide a 'varied' but man-made scene in a gentleman's park. The description, like most of Scott's, is exhaustively informative, with its detailed list of trees. Again, we notice the underlying interest in agriculture, in the human usefulness of the landscape.

Scott proceeds to appraise the scene more exactly. The italics are ours.

> Yet, though thus *embellished*, the scene could neither be strictly termed *sublime* or *beautiful*, and scarcely even *picturesque* or *striking*. But its extreme solitude pressed on the heart; the traveller felt that uncertainty whither he was going, or in what so wild a path was to terminate, which, at times, *strikes more on the imagination* than the *grand* features of a *show scene*, when you know the exact distance of *the inn where your dinner is bespoke*, and at the moment preparing.
>
> Ch. 2

In fact, to the roles of the historian and entertainer, Scott added that of the travel writer, using the jargon of the day to do the job performed by coloured photographs in a modern travel-agent's brochure. Like an honest agent, Scott told the tourists exactly what they would get for their trouble. In his beloved Border, he can promise only 'solitude', though he hints that the inns are ready to give the traveller a warm welcome.

THE WEIGHT OF DETAIL

The same fanatical concern for detail is found in Scott's descriptions of people and events. But here it is rarely niggling, and almost always significant. The elaborate description of the terrain of a battle which Scott will give us beforehand makes the fighting, when it starts, all the more swift and vivid. And the careful account of a man's clothes and features is basic to Scott's methods of characterisation, while it is also used to make important historical points.

The Talisman is not one of Scott's best novels, but the whole of its first chapter would be well worth quoting in illustration of this last point. It opens with a very powerful description, entirely concocted from books, of the Dead Sea and the landscape around it, through which we see a 'knight of the Red Cross' toiling: 'Upon this scene of desolation the sun shone with almost intolerable splendour, and all living nature seemed to have hidden itself from the rays, excepting the solitary figure which moved through the flitting sand at a foot's pace.' Then the camera (as it were) moves from this panoramic view into close-up: 'The dress of the rider, and the accoutrements of his horse, were peculiarly unfit for the traveller in such a country.' The knight's armour is painstakingly described, and each additional item hammers this last point home. His 'coat of linked mail', his 'steel breastplate', the 'cumbrous cylindrical helmet', the 'flexible mail' round his legs and thighs; the weight is intolerable to imagine. His 'surcoat of embroidered cloth' is 'much frayed and worn', so that his coat-of-arms can barely be made out, and his shield is so battered that the arms are barely legible there either. This is not romantic detail; it is real armour, which has been used till it is shabby.

Then Scott makes his historical point, rising naturally out of what he has shown us: 'In retaining their own unwieldy defensive armour, the northern Crusaders seemed to set at defiance the nature of the climate and the country to which they had come to war.' The Crusader soon meets a Saracen warrior, with his 'turban, long spear, and green caftan floating in the wind', and his light shield. Sir Kenneth has the better of the contest, but the point is well made that the Saracen's equipment is far more suited to 'the nature of the climate and the country'. Throughout the book, the Christian knights will figure as clumsy intruders, backward in comparison with their learned and gallant adversary, Saladin. Their code of chivalry will be exposed as hypocrisy; their Christianity will be seen as the façade concealing a lust for conquest.

The opening descriptions not only show us that the knights have really no business to be in Palestine, they also give us, almost ironically, the character of the hero, Sir Kenneth. For this armour suits Sir Kenneth, who is the most thick-headed of all the Crusaders; so dense, in fact, that he still stands by the principles of chivalry which his gallant leader, Coeur de Lion, is quite ready to discard when it suits him. After reading that first description, we could never imagine Sir Kenneth to be gay or quick-witted. Instead, his qualities of courage, stubbornness and loyalty are hinted at by his slow pace and his ponderous gear.

This is typical of Scott's presentation of his 'serious' characters—his historical figures and his 'dark heroes' (such as Fergus MacIvor and Burley). He is interested in their psychology, but he presents them as typical rather than individual people. The fascinating and convincing account which he gives us of the conflict between love and ambition in the Earl of Leicester, in *Kenilworth*, is built up partly through generalised language, partly through close observation of the man's appearance, speech and actions. It is significant that Scott habitually couches Leicester's private thoughts as soliloquies, a practice which he follows with other 'serious' characters, and with heroes like Henry Morton. Unlike later novelists, he is always polite about entering a man's mind, and a pair of inverted commas is his way of knocking on the door.

His 'serious' characters are usually seen from the outside, and they never develop. When we meet them, they are mature men and women who have reached their final stage of development already. We are introduced to Prince David of Rothsay, in *The Fair Maid of Perth*, who is one of Scott's best pictures of a complex personality, from the point of view of a casual bystander. A 'gallant young cavalier' appears

> on a noble Arabian horse, which he managed with exquisite grace, though by such slight handling of the reins, such imperceptible pressure of the limbs and sway of the body, that to any eye save that of an experienced horseman, the animal seemed to be putting forth his paces for his own amusement, and thus gracefully bearing forward a rider who was too indolent to give himself any trouble about the matter.

This hint of his horsemanship introduces us to the best and worst of Rothsay; he is gifted, but his laziness is both apparent and real. The paragraph of formal description which follows confirms this impression:

> The Prince's apparel, which was very rich, was put on with slovenly carelessness, His form, though his stature was low and his limbs extremely slight, was elegant in the extreme, and his features no less handsome. But there was on his brow a haggard paleness, which seemed the effect of care and dissipation, or of both these wasting causes combined. His eyes were sunk and dim, as from late indulgence in revelry on the preceding evening, while his cheek was inflamed with unnatural red, as if either the effect of the Bacchanalian orgies had not passed away from the constitution, or a morning draught had been resorted to, in order to remove the effects of the night's debauchery. Ch. 11

We are to see Rothsay in many aspects—as a clever counsellor, a drunken rake, a shamefaced liar, and, finally, a figure of great pathos. Everything is there already in the first description.

Like his contemporaries, Scott placed great reliance on a man's facial appearance, his 'physiognomy', as a way of judging his character. When Frank Osbaldistone, in *Rob Roy*, has seen MacVittie, his father's main correspondent in Glasgow, he remarks, 'There was something so singularly repulsive in the hard features of the Scotch trader, that I could not resolve to put myself in his hands without transgressing every caution which could be derived from the rules of physiognomy.' Moral attributes and characteristics, according to these 'rules', appear in the lines and features of the face—we still have the habit of saying 'he has a weak chin' or 'she has a weak mouth'. Scott often analyses a man's psychology through his face.

But other guides are important besides physiognomy. Dress (as in the case both of Sir Kenneth and of Rothsay) is useful. When Alan Fairford, in *Redgauntlet*, first meets Nanty Ewart, whom he knows as the captain of a smuggling brig, he is surprised to find that the man is *not* a 'typical' smuggler, but is dressed in a 'shabby genteel' way. Nanty, as he later explains to Alan, is an educated man from a middle-class background; but he has been a sailor for years, and there is no reason why he should not now dress like other smugglers. Scott (perhaps crudely in this case) uses dress to symbolise the man. Nanty is a good-hearted young man who has gone to waste—his 'tarnished lace', 'faded embroidery' and 'sullied sword belt' are signs both of a fall in status and a fall from grace.

Nanty, however, is an amalgamation of two types. He is a young profligate of the type which 18th-century writers were fond of shaking their heads over. (Robertson in *The Heart of Midlothian* is another.) But he is also a good sailor, who 'could steer through the Pentland Firth though he were as drunk as the Baltic Ocean'. Scott is more interested than any other British novelist, before or since, in what his characters do for a living, and how it moulds, deforms or exhibits their personalities. Here is a further guide to character.

OCCUPATIONS

When Scott portrays Jeanie Deans, it is not as a generalised 'lower-class' type, but as a particular type—the independent cow-feeder. So her letters home are full of comments on the English cattle, and the Duke of Argyle's interest in cheese gives him something in common with her. Scott is sometimes too rigid in making his characters look on the world from the point of view of their own profession. Eric Scambester, the butler in Magnus Troil's household in *The Pirate*, is asked why he prefers the pirate, Cleveland, to the hero, Mordaunt, and replies, 'Master Mordaunt is all for wan water, like his old dog-fish of a father; now Captain Cleveland, d'ye see, takes his glass, like an honest fellow and a gentleman.' This is too crude, but there is abundant truth-to-life in Andrew Fairservice, the gardener's, remark that 'a kail-blaid, or a colliflour, glances sae glegly by moonlight, it's like a leddy in her diamonds'; or in Meg Merrilies's 'professional pleasure' in laying out a dead body. ('He's a bonny corpse,' she muttered to herself, 'and weel worth the streaking.') No one is more ready than Scott to write about disinterested emotions like loyalty and compassion; but no one sees more clearly how every trade must impose certain attitudes to life in those who follow it. An armourer cannot oppose war.

The word 'ethos' is useful here, together with its adjective, 'ethical'. The 'professional ethos' or 'code' is the attitude shared by members of the learned professions. It is 'unethical' for one lawyer to compete with another or to betray his client's confidences. It would also be bad for the profession, and would work against the lawyers' interests. So within the very different ethical code of the world of business in general, we have this nobler-sounding 'ethos'.

Scott sees that even smugglers and outlaws have their ethical codes. Dirk Hatteraick, the ethical smuggler, looks on Glossin, the dishonourable lawyer, with contempt. The ethos of the clans, again, is radically different from that of modern society; it is all right to murder a man in a blood-feud, but criminal to refuse hospitality to a stranger.

Scott, at his best, is not a 'moral' writer presenting characters in terms of one fixed standard of good and evil—the Ten Commandments, say. Some ethical codes are, of course, richer and finer than others. But if a man is true to his own ethic, Scott does not blame him. Dugald Dalgetty, the mercenary soldier, is ready to change sides in war to get higher pay or better conditions. But at the end we see him refusing to break a contract to one side before its term expires, even at the risk of his own neck.

So a character in Scott—even a 'serious' character like Claverhouse—may be both right and wrong, heroic and evil, wise and stupid, depending on whether he is judged by his own code or that of others. This is important both in Scott's comic writing and his portrayal of history—indeed, it is what makes his comic writing historical and his history comic. And it makes our distinction between 'serious' and 'comic' characters very arbitrary. Cromwell and Rob Roy are both. So is King Louis in *Quentin Durward*.

THE COMEDY OF IDENTITY

At the beginning of the novel, Quentin runs into a man dressed like 'the merchant or shopkeeper of the period'. His physiognomy is described in typical fashion. 'The expression of this man's countenance was partly attractive, and partly forbidding. His strong features, sunk cheeks and hollow eyes had, nevertheless, an expression of shrewdness and humour congenial to the character of the young adventurer. But then, those same sunken eyes, from under the shroud of thick black eyebrows, had something in them that was at once commanding and sinister.' Quentin is befriended by this puzzling person. Later, he suddenly meets 'Maître Pierre' again—but this time as King Louis of France. 'But those eyes, which, according to Quentin's former impression, only twinkled with the love of gain, had, now that they were known to be the property of an able and powerful monarch, a piercing and majestic glance; and those wrinkles on the brow, which he had supposed were formed during a long series of petty schemes of commerce, seemed now the furrows which sagacity had worn while toiling in meditation upon the fate of nations.'

Quentin is right both times. Louis is not only an ally of the French merchants, he has many of the attitudes of the merchant. He remains throughout a thoroughly ambiguous character—callous, superstitious and deceitful, but also witty, wise and in some ways brave. Quentin's mistake is put to good comic effect, but this 'comedy of identity' also makes a valid historical point.

The most brilliant example of Scott's ability to see the same character from two different points of view occurs in *Redgauntlet*. The early part of the novel consists of 'letters' between the romantic Darsie Latimer, touring in the Border country, and the sober Alan Fairford, studying law in Edinburgh. Both meet Redgauntlet early in the book, but neither we nor they are sure that they are seeing the same man.

Darsie is strolling on the dangerous Solway Sands when he sees a number of horsemen spearing a salmon. The most expert of them is 'a tall man, well mounted on a strong black horse, which he caused to turn and wind like a bird in the air'. He acts like their leader, with 'striking gestures' and an 'uncommonly sonorous and commanding' voice. He soon intervenes to rescue Darsie from the tide. To Darsie, he seems a sinister yet noble figure; he compares him to ancient heroes, to 'Coriolanus, standing by the hearth of Tullus Aufidius' or 'Marius, seated among the ruins of Carthage.'

When Redgauntlet turns up in Edinburgh, Alan sees him as

an odd, 'rather elderly' man, in dress which, 'though it had once been magnificent, was now antiquated and unfashionable'. His haughty attitude outrages Alan. 'While my father said grace, the Laird did all but whistle aloud; and when I, at my father's desire, returned thanks, he used his toothpick, as if he had waited that moment for its exercise.'

Both first impressions are true to Redgauntlet's character, which we see only from the outside. He *is* a 'rather elderly man', but he is also a brilliant horseman in the prime of life. He is a sinister, dangerous and masterful character, a hero in the classic mould—but he is also a rude and pathetic eccentric, in out-of-date, square-toed shoes. In his own backward part of Scotland he is still a leader among men; in Edinburgh, he is a misfit.

Scott's best serious characters, then, are both good and bad, weak and strong, heroic and, at least potentially, comic. They are part of society and part of history; so their qualities strike different social groups in different ways, and they can only be judged in terms of their place in the development of history.

HEROES AND VILLAINS

Between the 'serious', or 'serio-comic' and the 'comic' or 'comico-serious' (to prate like Polonius for a moment), lie Scott's 'neutral' heroes and his 'moral' villains.

The role of Scott's heroes has been described already. In the early novels they are deliberately made pale and uninteresting beside the people they meet: but Scott's art developed later, and both Quentin Durward and Harry Gow are 'serio-comic' characters, realistic historical figures in their own right.

Waverley, Frank Osbaldistone, Brown, Lovel, Ivanhoe, are not quite colourless, but their personalities have virtually no influence on the course of the novels in which they appear except in one important respect—almost everyone likes them. They inspire a dog-like devotion in 'faithful followers' like Richie Moniplies and Gurth. When they are sick, imprisoned, condemned to death or threatened with murder, there is always a friend at hand to save them. Like Frank Osbaldistone, they find themselves 'driving, without a compass, on the ocean of human life'. Sometimes their passivity is quite extraordinary. Ivanhoe is sick during most of the novel which bears his name, but the activities of Locksley, Coeur de Lion, Rebecca, Gurth and Wamba ensure that he will emerge in safety to marry his heiress.

The heroines tend to be still more passive and colourless. One may except the mischievous Julia Mannering, and Di Vernon in *Rob Roy*, who is a charming tomboy on the lines of Shakespeare's Rosalind or Viola. Otherwise, there is a dire succession of young women whose names are hard to remember offhand and who say and do little or nothing of any interest or importance. For some of them—Rowena, for instance—Scott seems to have neither affection nor much respect.

But Rebecca, in the same novel, is vigorous and touching. She is monotonously good, but the whiff of the East which she carries about her adds colour to her nobility, and we really care what happens to her. An American critic, Alexander Welsh, has pointed out that it is typical of Scott to have a pair of contrasted heroines in this way: Flora and Rose in *Waverley*, Minna and Brenda Troil in *The Pirate*. There are dark-haired, often 'tragic', heroines, who are active and interesting (Di Vernon is dark), and fair-haired nobodies who usually marry the hero. The hero is attracted to both, but plumps for the safer, fair-haired one. The 'dark heroines' are matched with 'dark heroes'—Fergus MacIvor, Brian de Bois Guilbert, the pirate Cleveland. These, unlike the 'fair heroes', are very active men. We can extend this category, if we like, to cover other stern, active and violent men in the novels—Burley, Rob Roy, Redgauntlet. The first such character, it is worth pointing out, is the attractive yet guilty Marmion in Scott's second long poem.

It is the exception, rather than the rule, to get a complete foursome of fair and dark heroes and heroines, and Welsh's point must not be pressed too far. Anyway, the idea of contrasting heroines in this way is at least as old as Shakespeare's comedies. The pattern breaks down in most of the later novels. But it does help us to arrange our ideas about Scott. We see, for instance, that *The Bride of Lammermoor* is tragic because the fair heroine falls in love with a passionate and violent 'dark hero', Ravenswood, and cannot live up to his demands, and this fits into Scott's important theme of violence *versus* peace. When Waverley marries the pleasant Rose rather than the heroic Flora, he is plumping for peace. One of the troubles with *Rob Roy* is that we cannot imagine the rather spineless Frank attracting such a lively and fanatical girl as Di Vernon.

In his best plots, Scott does without wicked villains; history throws up the dark forces which threaten the hero, and it is the clash of ethics and classes which provides the action. When Scott does give us a villain, he is often no more interesting than the hero, and he tends to talk much more. *Kenilworth* gives us the full range of Scott's villains. There is the master-mind type, Varney, a clever and ambitious man whose hold over Leicester is well presented, but who is too consistently wicked to be credible. There is the alchemist, Alasco—one of several portraits in Scott of malicious men of 'science'. Antony Foster and the ruffian Lambourne are more interesting. Foster is a convincing hypocrite—a pseudo Puritan who has actually come to believe the hell-fire doctrines he professes, and is determined that his daughter will be saved from the devil. Lambourne, like many of Scott's ruffians, hovers on the edge of being fully sympathetic.

GYPSIES, BEGGARS AND SEERS

Far more important than the villains are the gallery of gypsies, seers, beggars, blind musicians, fortune-tellers and other strange figures standing on or outside the verge of civilised society. Their role in the Scottish novels is very important—Meg Merrilies and Edie Ochiltree, Norna of the Fitful Head and Wandering Willie, Madge Wildfire and Allan McAulay, Davie Gellatley and Blind Alice, varied though they are in their temperaments, have similar work to do. They introduce the possibility of uncanny happenings; they sing or play appropriate songs and tunes; they make prophecies of fatal events and strange destinies. They represent the dying folk-traditions of the old countryside, reminding us that the land is older than the people who now live in it. Madge Wildfire's songs hark back to the ballads; Blind Alice is a feudal intrusion into the new, commercial world of the Ashtons.

Scott needs wily, earthy characters like Meg and Edie to sort out his cumbersome plots. Their ears are close to the ground, and they travel fast across the country they know so well to help the hero. Also, like Alice and Allan, such figures can comment on the 'new men' from the point of view of the 'old world'. Scott sometimes provides figures in the non-Scottish novels to do similar jobs. The loyal Wamba risks his life for his master, and makes cutting jests even about Coeur de Lion himself. The Bohemian, in *Quentin Durward*, master-minds part of the plot.

COMIC CHARACTERS

The great body of Scott's characters, however, are neither great men, nor heroes, nor villains, nor prophets. The temptation is to describe them all as 'comic' characters. Some, like the Mucklebackits in *The Antiquary*, live through the miseries of the poor; others, like Caleb Balderstone in *The Bride of Lammermoor*, are pathetic as well as funny; and others still, like Ephraim McBriar in *Old Mortality* and Evan Dhu in *Waverley*, rise to heroic status at their deaths. But they are all seen with the same impartial, sympathetic yet laughing eye. Scott's method with these 'comico-serious' characters is always much the same. He describes them, gives them their place in society and history, and then lets them talk. Once they have started talking they amuse us or move us. Without always realising it themselves, they make ironic comments on their neighbours and on society at large. They reveal their own simplicity or hypocrisy or greed. Even those novels which come close to true 'tragedy'—*The Bride of Lammermoor* and *Kenilworth*—are largely taken up with the comedies of the common life of the period in which they are set. When we think of the gloomy Ravenswood brooding at Wolf's Crag, we simultaneously remember the witty scene in which Caleb steals the cooper's dinner.

Scott's comedy, like all great comedy, is essentially serious. It reflects a balanced and humane outlook, not a flippant one.

It is also essentially historical. When people from different classes, with different codes of behaviour, are thrown together by historical upheavals, the results may be grave, or comic, or even both. Besides this, in Scott's broad perspective of history and society, the outlooks and actions of ordinary people, which are limited by the time and place they live in, are bound to seem either touching or funny. So there are two main types of comedy in Scott; the 'comedy of collision', between widely different types of people, and the 'comedy of self-exposure', when people show themselves up by their deeds and conversation.

For examples of 'the comedy of collision' (of which the 'comedy of identity', already discussed, is one type), one might take the hilarious conversation between Dugald Dalgetty and the wild Highlander, Ranald McEagh, in the Duke of Argyle's dungeon, when the two men simply cannot understand each other at all, yet are bound together in comradeship by their situation. Or there is the fine moment in *Old Mortality* when Cuddie Headrigg, the wily ploughman, is on trial for his life for his own small part in the Covenanters' rebellion. His judges are the notorious tyrants, the Duke of Lauderdale and General Dalzell.

> 'Were you at the battle of Bothwell Brigg?' was the first question which was thundered in his ears.
>
> Cuddie meditated a denial, but had sense enough, upon reflection, to discover that the truth would be too strong for him; so he replied, with true Caledonian indirectness of response, 'I'll no say but it may be possible that I might hae been there.'
>
> 'Answer directly, you knave—yes, or no? You know you were there.'
>
> 'It's no for me to contradict your Lordship's Grace's honour,' said Cuddie.
>
> 'Once more, sir, were you there?—yes, or no?' said the Duke impatiently.
>
> 'Dear stir,' again replied Cuddie, 'how can ane mind preceesely where they hae been a' the days of their life?'
>
> 'Speak out, you scoundrel,' said General Dalzell, 'or I'll dash your teeth out with my dudgeonhaft.' . . . Ch. 36

Scott does not falsify life by making these terrible trials an occasion for comedy. He does not attempt to mitigate Dalzell's brutality. But the comedy is implicit in the collision, and the dialogue would be equally funny even if Cuddie were later executed.

Another type of 'the comedy of collision' occurs when the inimitable Richie Moniplies describes to his master, Nigel, his unfortunate encounter with James VI and I.

> '. . . And down, sir, came the King, with all his nobles, dressed out in his hunting suit of green, doubly laced, and laid down with gowd. I minded the very face o' him, though it was lang since I saw him. But my certie, lad, thought I, times are changed since ye came fleeing down the backstairs of auld Holyrood House, in grit fear, having your breeks in your hand without time to put them on . . .' Ch. 3

To hear a serving man describing the King with such familiarity is amusing for two reasons. First of all, it reminds us that the King is only a man, who has been seen without his trousers on occasion, and the dissonance between our dignified idea of kingship and the human dimension to it creates laughter. Secondly, Richie sees James as only another Edinburgh lad, like himself, who has made good in the world—and this is the 'comedy of self-exposure'. Richie reveals his own conceit.

Scott was an excellent mimic in 'real life', and his gift for differentiating the speech of his various characters is akin to mimicry. The mimic does not give us the man—Harold Wilson, say—as he really is. He exaggerates leading traits and makes the speech far more self-revealing than it would be in reality. Scott is not a 'naturalistic' writer, copying the dull way in which most people usually talk. He is a realist, who sets out to give us characters typical of the classes, trades and varieties of men as they really are. Cuddie is a typical Clydesdale ploughman—notice how Scott refers to his 'true [i.e. typical] Caledonian indirectness'. Scott makes Cuddie shrewd enough, brave enough, frank enough to be interesting; he is not an ordinary ploughman, but someone who takes the ploughman's traits to the heights.

Scott gives him enough bad grammar to be true to his upbringing, but not so much that he is incomprehensible.

Scott set out to do for the Scots what Maria Edgeworth had done for the Irish, that is, to explain them to other peoples. He fastened on certain typical Scots traits which occur again and again in his characters and which are still easily recognised in Scotsmen today. Drunkenness is one. Religious fanaticism is another. Pride of lineage and local patriotism together form a third—Scott quotes the French expression, '*fier comme un Écossais*'. Pedantry and argumentativeness compose a fourth trait.

None of these traits is accidental; the Scottish character developed, as Scotts show, out of the climate, the ruggedness, the poverty of the country. To take pedantry as an example; John Knox's Reformation in Scotland made the Scots the best educated people in Europe. The preacher was also the village schoolmaster, and few families were so poor that they could not hope to send a bright son to university, to become a preacher in his turn.

So Scott gives us a formidable range of pedants, all the way from James I, 'the wisest fool in Christendom', down to Andrew Fairservice, who piques himself on knowing the Latin names of the plants which he tends.

Fairservice, like many of Scott's best comic characters, is a hybrid of several 'types'. He is a pedant; he is a typical gardener, who loves his work; he is a local patriot who thinks everything in Scotland better than its equivalent in England; he is a 'loyal follower', an opinionated serving-man out of the same stable as Richie Moniplies; finally, he is a religious bigot, who denounces the service in an English church as 'clauts o' cauld parritch—clauts o' cauld parritch'. It has been pointed out that he is an almost completely odious character, and yet we love him; the explanation is that we are delighted with this odd combination of 'typical' traits. In the same way, Baron Bradwardine, in *Waverley*, is a very funny and very moving compound of three favourite types—the genuine scholar, the hard-drinking, hospitable laird, and the idealistic cavalier. Scott can ring the changes on his types for ever without repeating himself.

To each Scottish-speaking character Scott gives his or her own rhythms and mannerisms. Among his religious extremists, there is a wide range from Douce Davie Deans's querulous, gossipy combination of the language of the Bible with the Scottish vernacular, to the heroic Burley's streamlined sermonising, with its hint of the idiom of the law, or the milder, more middle-class biblical speech of the Quaker, Joshua Geddes.

Contrast these two talkative women:

> '. . . there is nothing I would not do for the Lady of Avenel and her family, and that has been proved, and for her servants to boot, both Martin and Tibb, although Tibb is not so civil sometimes as altogether I have a right to expect; but I cannot think it beseeming to have angels, or ghosts, or fairies, or the like, waiting upon a leddy when she is in another woman's house, in respect it is in no ways creditable.' THE MONASTERY, Ch. 8

> 'Nabobs, indeed! the country's plagued wi' them. They have raised the price of eggs and pootry for twenty miles round.—But what is my business?—They use amaist a' of them the Well down by—they need it, ye ken, for the clearing of their copper complexions, that need scouring as much as my saucepans, that naebody can clean but mysell.' ST. RONAN'S WELL, Ch. 2

Both women stray off the point. But whereas the wanderings of the first are the involuntary results of a rather feeble mind, the second scores a bull's-eye every time she changes target: she is full of ideas. The difference in character, one might say, is the difference between the semi-colon which limply divides the first woman's chaotic sentence, and the emphatic periods, dashes and 'thats' which articulate the tirade of the second. Both provide the comedy of self-exposure. While the first lets her snobbish complaints against Tibb slip out almost by accident, the second is pleased with herself, and doesn't mind who knows it. Scott characterises his people not only by what they say and the words they use, but by the basic rhythms of their speech. (The first woman is Dame Glendinning in *The Monastery*; the second is the innkeeper, Meg Dods, in *St. Ronan's Well.*)

In his novels about the Middle Ages and Stewart England, Scott is compelled to forsake the Scots dialect he loved, and he creates a variety of synthetic languages. As he explains in an introduction to *Ivanhoe*, he believes that a historical novelist must try to capture the character of an 'ancient language' without puzzling the reader with the words actually used in those days.

The result, in *Ivanhoe*, is the bastard language which we know as 'Wardour-St. English'—'A truce to thy insolence, fellow' . . . 'Nay, by St. Mary, Brother Brian' . . . 'In truth, venerable father' . . . 'Tush'. No one ever talked like this, outside the historical fiction of Scott and his imitators. The language of *Kenilworth*, *The Fortunes of Nigel* and *Woodstock* is equally synthetic, though its borrowings from Shakespeare and other Elizabethan and Jacobean writers give it more surface liveliness. In *Woodstock*, Scott ranges further still for something to imitate, to Puritan pamphlets and Restoration plays. The results are not bad; with the comic characters, we soon cease to be conscious of the imitation. But even the best of them lack that individuality which we find in the Scottish novels.

Giles Gosling, in *Kenilworth*, talks a tidied-up and modernised version of the language of Shakespeare's comedies:

> 'This peevish humour of melancholy sits ill upon you—it suits not with a sleek boot, a hat of a trim block, a fresh cloak, and a full purse—A pize on it, send it off to those who have their legs swathed with a hay-wisp, their heads thatched with a felt bonnet, their jerkin as thin as a cobweb and their pouch without ever a cross to keep the fiend Melancholy from dancing on it.' Ch. I

The trouble is that Shakespeare clearly heightened the speech and typified the characters of his comic figures just as Scott did. (There is a direct influence, of course; the way in which Scott constructs a long speech by Dugald Dalgetty, as well as elements in his character, remind us forcibly of Falstaff and Fluellen, just as Dickens learnt some of his comic tricks from Scott.) Giles Gosling is a type of a type. The rhythms of his speech are too even; the metaphors recall the rather feeble wit of the *Two Gentlemen of Verona*. Though Scott's synthetic speech often has more vigour than this—Wildrake in *Woodstock* is given real life—the characters who speak it are barer and cruder than his best Scotsmen.

The same applies to Scott's 'serious' characters, and his heroes. The best of them do have their own mannerisms, but the language itself is formal, and unresponsive to character. Di Vernon, on the one hand, is as individual in her rhythms as Meg Dods. But the duller heroes and heroines talk like this:

> 'Do not go there now,' said his sister. 'The house of our ancestors is at present the habitation of a wretch as insidious as dangerous, whose arts and villainy accomplished the ruin and broke the heart of our unhappy father.'
>
> 'You increase my anxiety,' replied the brother, 'to confront this miscreant, even in the den he has constructed for himself . . .'
>
> GUY MANNERING, Ch. 52

We know (from the conversations of Dr. Johnson, for instance), that educated people in the 18th century spoke much more formally than we do now. But, in the midst of violence and excitement, Scott's dimmer heroes pay as much attention to the construction of their sentences as to what is going on around them ('Are you not sensible of a smell of fire?'). The conversation above, between a brother and sister just reunited, is simply not human.

But there are times when Scott's 'serious' speech, and the speech of his comic characters in a serious moment, can reach real stature. These moments come when a character rises above himself to make a grand yet simple human statement, a prophecy or a curse. The noble language of some of Scott's Highlanders—Allan McAulay, for instance, in *Montrose*—often rings out with powerful, elemental poetic imagery, and with a deep and tragic dignity. Meg Merrilies's famous denunciation of the Laird of Ellangowan when he turns the gypsies out of their camp, rises far above mere 'stageyness'—or, at least, reminds us that 'the stage' covers Shakespeare and Aeschylus as well as third-rate melodrama. 'Ride your ways, Laird of Ellangowan—ride your ways, Godfrey Bertram!—This day have ye quenched seven smoking hearths—see if the fire in your ain parlour burn the blyther for that . . .' This type of speech, with its strong, surging rhythms and its hammering repetitions is the nearest Scott comes to 'fine writing', to prose artfully composed for a big effect.

Even better is the great testament which Scott gives to Claverhouse:

> 'But in truth, Mr. Morton, why should we care so much for death, light upon us or around us whenever it may? Men die daily—not a bell tolls the hour but it is the death note of someone or other; and why hesitate to shorten the span of others, or take over-anxious care to prolong our own? It is all a lottery—when the hour of midnight came, you were to die—it has struck, you are alive and safe, and the lot has fallen on those fellows who were to murder you. It is not the expiring pang that is worth thinking of in an event that must happen one day, and may befall us on any given moment—it is the memory which the soldier leaves behind him, like the long train of light that follows the sunken sun—that is all which is worth caring for, which distinguishes the death of the brave or the ignoble. When I think of death, Mr. Morton, as a thing worth thinking of, it is in the hope of pressing one day some well-fought and hard-won field of battle, and dying with the shout of victory in my ear—*that* would be worth dying for, and more, it would be worth having lived for.' OLD MORTALITY, Ch. 34

It is easy to see why Jeanie Deans's simple plea for her sister, another of Scott's great speeches, should be profoundly moving. But Claverhouse is not a sympathetic character. Why does this speech take our breath away?

In the first place, it is perfectly in character. Here is Claverhouse, cool and polished as ever, standing on a floor still slippery with the blood of yet more Covenanters whom his troops have slaughtered. He addresses the hero, with perfect formality, as 'Mr. Morton'; the dead men were 'those fellows'. The rhythms of the speech are prim yet flowing, taut yet varied, the natural expression of a subtle, clever man who is also a snob.

Secondly, we know that Claverhouse will die as he professes to wish, at Killiecrankie, and in a moment Habakkuk Mucklewrath will rise like a ghost before him and foretell that death in another overwhelming speech. This is the method of the epic; declamation and prophecy, an irony which would be tragic if life, in the epics, did not always go on.

Thirdly, Claverhouse, like Meg and Jeanie, rises above himself while remaining entirely himself. At this moment, he is a spokesman for all the merciless Cavaliers of Scotland's two generations of civil war. He is nobler than the worst of them, crueller than the best of them; he is, in fact, the supreme 'type', and yet the supreme individual. The confrontation of the doomed Claverhouse and the dying Habakkuk gives us the essence of a period, while both men, with their visions of the future, suddenly rise above history itself and command it. From the heart of a small event, a brief collision, Scott draws and distils the poetry of history.

7

Scott and History

Not all novels which are set in the past are about history. But almost all Scott's novels (even *The Antiquary*) have history itself as their subject. To look for self-contained treatment of individual 'moral' themes, as some foolish critics have done, is to misunderstand a Scott novel completely.

Two later writers who were influenced by Scott, George Eliot and Dickens, set novels in the past which were not 'about' history. *Barnaby Rudge* deals with a famous riot, like *The Heart of Midlothian*. Dickens introduces us to a 'real' historical figure, Lord George Gordon, but he shows no understanding of the social forces which raised Gordon to some prominence in the 1780s, nor of the difference between men of that time and those of his own day. In *Middlemarch*, in the same way, we do not feel that George Eliot is describing people of a different period from the one in which she herself wrote; yet she sets the novel 'forty years since', at the time of the 1832 Reform Bill, one of the landmarks of British history. The Reform Bill is, indeed, mentioned, but it is used as background, much as a writer today might set a modern love story at the period of the General Strike.

By contrast, history dominates *The Heart of Midlothian*. The riot which opens the book is presented as the natural outcome of the state of Scottish society in the 1730s, a direct result of the Act of Union with England thirty years before. It is because of the humiliating subservience of Scotland to England that Effie is so hardly dealt with and Jeanie must walk to London. It is because of her father's commitment to the Covenanting cause, and its influence on her own upbringing, that Jeanie cannot tell the lie which would save her sister's life. In fact, the novel carries on the sweep of Scottish history which opens with *Montrose*, continues in *Old Mortality*, *The Bride of Lammermoor*, *Rob Roy*, *Waverley* and *Redgauntlet* and ends more placidly in *Guy Mannering* and *The Antiquary*, which are set within Scott's own lifetime. Its subject, like theirs, is the transition of Scotland from a wild and backward country to a modern and prosperous one. Dugald Dalgetty, Cuddie Headrigg, Caleb Balderstone, Rob Roy, Fergus MacIvor, Meg Merrilies and Edie Ochiltree are, like Jeanie herself, people caught up in history, who represent certain social trends, certain types of character, thrown up by the transition.

Scott accepted the results of this historical transition, yet regretted them. This paradox is explained in our first chapter. While he welcomed new comfort and new prosperity, he mourned the collapse of feudalism, the destruction of the clans, the cessation of a whole type of heroism. He accepted, in his own life, the new capitalist relationships which replaced feudalism; but his imagination loved to dwell on the nobler features of the old orders of society. He conjures up a picture of the *community* which had above all been lost. The chieftain with his whole clan eating under him, and a bard on hand to sing its proud songs; the feudal lord dining in a great hall with his retainers; wars in which every able-bodied man was bound to fight side by side with his neighbours—these ways of life were lost, and the Edinburgh Volunteers and the oddities of Abbotsford could not make up for them.

Scott's Toryism was a real strength to him when he studied the past. He was ready to sympathise with whatever he found there, but the strength of his feeling for it ruled out sentimentality. If Claverhouse and Rob Roy were worth admiring, it was important to find out why their causes had failed. History was so personal to him that his curiosity plunged him into dusty old books and documents, and what he found there proved that the transition which he half-accepted, half-deplored, had been inevitable. His prejudices made the past live for him; his second thoughts gave him a truer picture of it. So Claverhouse, in *Old*

Mortality, is not an attractive man, though Scott doted on his memory.

TWO VIEWS OF HISTORY

The essence of his greatness is the way in which he shows us that the character and outlook of a human being are limited by the time and place in which he lives—his understanding of the 'ethics' of the past. Dalgetty can no more grasp the usefulness of bows and arrows to outlawed Highlanders than they can comprehend a mercenary soldier. 'Chivalry' is not an eternal human standard which we should aim at now; it was the ethic, largely composed of self-deception, of a particular class of men at a particular time. Only when we understand the difference between one style of life and another can we understand change; and only when we understand how life has changed in history can we understand how it may be changing in the present. This was Scott's breakthrough, revolutionary in his own time and impressive even now.

Scott himself never thought his way through to a clear understanding of his own historical lessons. As his 'moralising' asides often show, he half-shared the 18th-century view that human nature was a fixed thing, that the men of the past could be judged by the same standards as men of the present. At the beginning of *Waverley*, he promises to emphasise 'those passions common to men in all stages of society, and which have alike agitated the human heart, whether it throbbed under the steel corslet of the 15th century, the brocaded coat of the 18th, or the blue frock and white dimity waistcoat of the present day'. The novel which follows makes nonsense of this. Baron Bradwardine, an old-fashioned figure even in 1745, could not have existed in the Edinburgh of Scott's day. The heroism of Evan Dhu is of a type which only a primitive society could throw up. Yet Scott persisted in this theory, as the 'Dedicatory Epistle' to *Ivanhoe* shows.

And this moralising, static view of history does spoil his novels, especially at those (fortunately rare) moments when Scott begins to take his romantic plot seriously and tries to create a 'timeless' tragedy. *The Heart of Midlothian* is the saddest example of this. The moralised 'dark hero', Robertson/Staunton, is a 'timeless' character with no historical meaning, nothing to contribute to the theme of transition. His very, very unlikely death at the hands of his own son, born out of wedlock, is no doubt supposed to remind us of the tragic consequences of wrongdoing, but it makes a very poor close to such a book. True tragedy needs more than a few long rhetorical speeches and a handsome face; the character who fulfils it must have real stature, and when his weakness causes his death, we must believe it to be inevitable, or at least likely. Neither is true of Staunton, who spoils the book wherever he figures in it.

The Pirate is completely ruined by an outbreak of 'timeless' human nature. Norna of the Fitful Head begins as a counterpart to Meg Merrilies and Edie Ochiltree—a fortune-teller who embodies the old Norse customs and legends of the Shetlands. Then Scott changes his mind and tries to make her a tragic figure, maddened by an exotic and disastrous love-affair. The theme of the encroachment of new ways on the old life of the Shetlands is set aside (admittedly, Scott's treatment of it has never been very promising) and the novel collapses under a preposterous plot.

Scott reintroduced the word 'tush' as a medieval exclamation, and has often been accused of 'tushery'. By 'tushery' we mean the sort of nonsense which disfigures *The Pirate*. The novelist takes historical costumes and events and makes them the background to a sentimental or melodramatic love story which would not be out of place in a women's magazine. History is used only to provide 'local colour' and to make a predictable tale more attractive.

This rarely happens elsewhere in Scott. The love story draws the reader *into* history in novels as diverse as *Waverley* and *Kenilworth*. There are dreadful outbreaks of 'tushery' in many novels—the chemist Dwining in *The Fair Maid of Perth*, for example, a prototype of the mad scientist in some 'epic' Superman adventure, with his proneness to chuckle 'he-he-he', as he pours out yet another dread potion. But usually the historical interest of the novel is strong enough to survive them.

At his best Scott either makes his plot do a historical job of work, as in *Waverley* and *Redgauntlet*, or treats it light-heartedly. He pokes fun at himself in the mottoes he puts above his chapters, or he allows a minor figure to make deflating remarks about the romantic characters. In *Old Mortality* and *Quentin Durward*, he conjures up typical lady readers from the circulating libraries of the time when the moment comes to supply the happy ending. In *Old Mortality*, the news that all the good characters lived happily ever after is only divulged in response to earnest cross-questioning by Miss Martha Buskbody, and the whole idea of living happily ever after is made to seem as ridiculous as it really is. In *Quentin Durward*, Scott explains in the introduction that Louis XI is 'the principal character in the romance—for it will be easily comprehended that the little love intrigue of Quentin is only employed as the means of bringing out the story'. When Quentin is rewarded with his Countess at the end, Scott pretends in an epilogue that a lady has written to him asking for 'a precise and particular account of the espousals of the young heir of Glen-houlakin and the lovely Flemish Countess'. He refuses, pointing out that if he described what really went on at a 15th-century wedding, his genteel lady readers would be shocked out of their wits, and would think less of Isabelle de Croye than of 'the maid who milks, and does the meanest chores'. So much for eternal human nature.

So the meat of Scott's novels, in his opinion and ours, is the history. He is anxious to write fair and accurate history; but as he points out in the Dedicatory Epistle to *Ivanhoe*, a pedantically accurate historical novel would be unreadable. The mass of detail would be so great that we could neither understand nor enjoy it.

SCOTT'S REALISM

Just as Scott selects characters who represent trends and types, so he chooses details from the life of the past which will bring it alive without too much effort, and yet also make worth while historical points. Sir Kenneth's armour is interesting in itself, but also suggests a reason for the failure of the Crusade. Scott's frequent descriptions of meals are not only lively in their own right, but say something about the social position of the people who eat them. In *Guy Mannering*, we first see Dandie Dinmont devouring 'huge slices of cold boiled beef' washed down with 'a large tankard of ale'. This is simple food, but there is plenty of it; the Border country is backward, but Dandie is a prosperous farmer. Counsellor Pleydell, for all the coarseness which is part of his character, takes sauce with his 'brace of wild ducks'—this is the difference between Edinburgh and Liddesdale. Both types of fare contrast with Meg Merrilies's excellent gypsy stew, 'composed of fowls, hares, partridges and moorgame'. The stewpot is a natural method of cooking for a wandering people, for they can throw into it anything which comes their way, by theft or good fortune.

Or take the cooper's best room, in which he puts up the great Marquis in *The Bride of Lammermoor*. While the old feudal family of Ravenswood has lost everything but one uncomfortable castle, this middle-class man in the little village nearby has been rising in the world. The room shows us that he has pretensions—he puts stamped leather on his walls like 'the inferior landholders and clergy'. The merry fire is 'composed of old pitch-barrel staves'—that is, of the by-products of the cooper's trade. There is linen of 'most fresh and dazzling whiteness on the bed', and—a devastating detail this—the 'old fashioned mirror' on the toilette beside the bed was 'part of the dispersed finery of the neighbouring castle'. There is plenty to eat and drink during the night—the room seems 'victualled against a siege of two or three days'.

Nothing could be further from mere 'tushery' or 'local colour'. The contrast between the comfort of this home and the complete lack of it in Ravenswood's castle, of which we have been made vividly and persistently aware by now, is rammed home in detail after detail. Not only is the cooper well-provided with necessaries, he can afford to imitate the luxury of his social superiors, and can rise to providing new linen on the bed. The victory of the rising middle class over the old feudal landlord is symbolised by that mirror which the cooper has bought at the sale of Ravenswood's furniture. So this mass of details embodies not only the contrast between two styles of life, but the rise of one class and the fall of another.

This is what we mean when we call Scott a 'realistic' writer. He does not merely describe the surface of life, he shows us what was really going on underneath it. We do not know what are the most significant events of our own days. In two hundred years' time, the Japanese victories in the Far East in 1942 may seem far more significant than Britain's part in the defeat of Nazism, because of their effect on colonial peoples. The 'realistic' historical novelist, then, cannot show history exactly as his characters saw it. He must select the incidents and types of people who pointed the way forward. Baillie Nicol Jarvie is a 'signpost', in *Rob Roy*, pointing to the future. At a time when most Scotsmen are in two minds about the Union with England, or oppose it, the Baillie speaks enthusiastically in its favour. That is why Frank Osbaldistone has to go to Glasgow, as well as the Highlands, because that was the town which prospered most swiftly and directly from the Union. Without the Baillie, *Rob Roy* would be unhistorical, because the direction of change would not emerge clearly from it.

Scott's realism depends on detail, but it does not call for pedantic accuracy. If every item in the cooper's best room turned out to be anachronistic, that would not make the description any the less true to history. In *Ivanhoe*, Scott, partly consciously but partly unwittingly, has telescoped several hundred years of English history into the short reign of Coeur de Lion. While Ulrica evokes the barbarism of the dark ages, De Bracy, with his mercenary troops, brings us close to the world of Dugald Dalgetty. Many details are wildly anachronistic. The Castle of Coningsburgh, for instance, was *not* Saxon. But *Ivanhoe* gives a broadly realistic picture of a period of historical change. It is, if you like, one of Scott's 'case studies' around his favourite theme of Jacobitism. 'Saxon nationalism' of Cedric's type is bound to fail; yet out of the intermingling of Norman and Saxon which the novel shows to be inevitable, came the English language and English history.

Scott never makes the mistake, common in his day and ours, of imagining that history is a list of kings and battles. Great men and great events are rare. When they arrive, it is because the state of society calls for them. When Cromwell first appears, well after the beginning of *Woodstock*, we know that this great man has not created the revolution. The revolution has been produced by forces outside the control of any one man; its course has made men look to Cromwell for leadership, because of his combination of gifts. The poverty of the Highlands, which Edward Waverley sees on his first visit to Tully Veolan, is an essential basis for the 1745 Rebellion. The distance from the squalor of the straggling village to the gaiety of Prince Charlie's court at Edinburgh is a great one, but when we see the Pretender for the first time, we already know why so many Scotsmen were prepared to risk what little they had for him.

When he does concentrate attention on his great men, Scott remains a master of realism. Two very good passages in particular stand out as models of how to handle court politics in fiction. One is the sequence where Louis XI bluffs and bribes and flatters and jokes his way out of the clutches of his rival, Charles the Bold of Burgundy, laying the basis for future successes when he seems doomed to final failure. The other is the long section of *Kenilworth* which deals with the dissensions of Elizabeth's court. Again, history is telescoped—all the people whom Scott mentions could not have been flourishing there at the same time. But Scott keeps us on tenterhooks while Leicester, Sussex and their parties manœuvre round the Queen. (Amy Robsart's fate depends on the result of the quarrel, and this holds our attention firmly.) He shows us how it is in Elizabeth's (and England's) interest that no powerful courtier should become completely predominant. Leicester, while self-seeking courtiers flatter him because they hope to rise to power and riches in his pockets, is compelled to flatter in his turn—not only Elizabeth herself, but also the tradesmen, officials and poets on whom his popularity and his chances depend. Here he is passing out of the court after his unexpected victory over Sussex.

> 'Poynings, good morrow, and how does your wife and fair daughter? Why come they not to court?—Adams, your suit is naught—the Queen will grant no more monopolies—but I may serve you in another matter.—My good Alderman Aylford, the suit of the City, affecting Queenhithe, shall be forwarded as far as my poor interest can serve—Master Edmund Spenser, touching your Irish petition, I would willingly aid you, from my love to the Muses; but thou hast nettled the Lord Treasurer.' KENILWORTH, Ch. 17

Scott takes the great themes of history to the heart of the common life, to Cuddie Headrigg and his mother, to the cooper at Wolf's Crag. Or, as in this case, he takes the common life to the heart of a great court full of famous names. Either way, we can never forget that both go forward at the same time, and that each depends on the other.

'Bothwell Brig 1679' is an important date of Scottish history, which gets at least a couple of lines in the swiftest survey of the nation's past. Only 5,000 'Covenanters' were actually up in arms, but they mostly came from the significant area round Glasgow, which was to take over the domination of Scotland's economic life. It was not just an episode in the career of 'Bluidy Clavers', nor a victory for one religious creed over another. It was part of the struggle against feudalism and the absolute monarchy. Forgotten men of all classes fought on both sides. Douce Davie Deans fought alongside Baillie Nichol Jarvie's father. On the other side were Sir Robert Redgauntlet and Lord Ravenswood with their feudal retainers. The reverberations of Bothwell Brig run through a whole cycle of Scott's novels, right down to the lovable Whig Antiquary himself. But we chiefly feel them through the lives of people who left no individual mark on history.

SCOTT'S THEMES IN 'REDGAUNTLET'

Redgauntlet, which deals with a small-scale, abortive (and wholly invented) attempt by Bonnie Prince Charlie to regain the throne of Britain, years after the '45, might hardly seem to be a historical novel at all. Scott sets it in the period just before his own birth. Prince Charlie, a shadow of his youthful self, is the only 'real' person to appear for more than a few moments. There is only one 'event' in the novel, an attack by the fishermen of the Solway Firth on the nets which the Quaker, Joshua Geddes, has erected. But two ripples on the sea of human life—a mismanaged plot and a riot, both taking place in a backward and isolated corner of Britain—give Scott enough material for his profoundest treatment of history.

The riot contains much history in little. The nets—which catch more fish more economically—threaten the old-fashioned fisheries of the local inhabitants. They are an intrusion of modern capitalism into the traditional way of life. The middle-class burghers, whose early struggles with their feudal overlords feature in *The Fair Maid of Perth* and *Quentin Durward*, have now extended their methods even into the Border Country. Joshua Geddes stands for a whole class of 'new men' and their system. Like Nichol Jarvie, he is a signpost—one of the very last on the way to Scott's own lifetime.

Redgauntlet himself is trying to turn back the tide of history. In place of the new world of the polished young Edinburgh lawyer Alan Fairford (who can't understand why his own father tolerates Redgauntlet's rudeness), he wants the old world of Wandering Willie. In place of the Hanoverian kings, who have let the representatives of property and commercial interests run the nation, he wants the Stewarts, with their stubborn and destructive belief in their absolute, God-given right to rule as they please. In place of the peace which has settled on Scotland after centuries of feuds and civil war, he wants violent rebellion. Like all the Redgauntlets before him, he is making a firm stand for the losing side.

In this novel, Scott's minor themes, which we find recurring within his major theme of historical development, are all brought together, quietly, subtly, brilliantly.

There is the theme of peace versus war. Over and over again in his novels he asks whether his own passion for violence is justified. Is it better to take arms and fight for a cause, rather than keeping out of harm's way? Claverhouse says 'yes'; Cuddie Headrigg says 'I have to', but Morton says that he can never be reconciled to the bloodshed which he sees around him. He is the signpost.

In *The Fair Maid of Perth*, Scott describes a chaotic kingdom, and sets the peace-loving heroine, Catherine Glover, against the headstrong, aggressive hero, Harry Gow, As individuals they come to terms with each other; Harry Gow, after joining in the horribly bloodthirsty battle of the two clans on the North Inch of Perth, is sick of slaughter. Catherine comes to realise that, in a turbulent age, she should be grateful to have a lover who is ready and able to defend her. Her mentor, the peaceful Father Clement, is born out of his time.

In the same way, the Covenanters are bound to take up arms, as Morton does, to defend their rights against tyranny; and Rob Roy can only make a violent answer to unjust laws. But by the period of *Waverley*, as Scott sees it, the case for violence is breaking down. Waverley himself marries the peaceful Rose, not the warlike Flora. He is proud of his military career, but his attitude to it is symbolised by the painting which he hangs up on the wall of the house at Tully Veolan. There are Edward and MacIvor at the head of the clan—but they are stuck to the canvas now, and will never march out of it again. What began as a passionate struggle for a cause ends as a literally 'picturesque' touch to the furnishings of a dining parlour.

Scott's mature attitude to strife was that it was sometimes necessary and inevitable, but never desirable for its own sake. Those who think of Scott as an unthinking upholder of chivalry, should re-read his account of the tournament in *Ivanhoe*. He ends with bitter Swiftian irony by giving the numbers of the dead ('including one who was smothered by the heat of his armour'), the dying and the disabled: '. . . And those who escaped best carried the marks of the conflict to the grave with them. Hence it is always mentioned in the old records, as the Gentle and Joyous Passage of Arms at Ashby.' (Though Scott, of course, was well aware that the adjectives carried a different meaning in the Middle Ages.)

The theme of peace versus strife shades, in the medieval novels, into the theme of kingship. For all his attractive qualities, Coeur de Lion is portrayed in both *Ivanhoe* and *The Talisman* as a rash and incompetent king, who should be looking after the interests of his people at home, not waging hopeless Crusades in search of military glory for himself. Louis XI, on the other hand, is an unpleasant man who makes his own daughter miserable and is ready to execute anyone who thwarts him. Yet he, not the chivalrous Charles the Bold, is the model for kingship, as is Elizabeth in *Kenilworth*, who suppresses her resentment against Leicester's betrayal of her womanly feelings in the interests of her kingdom. These intelligent, peaceable monarchs are contrasted with the long and usually disastrous line of Stewarts.

So the theme of kingship marries with that of the Good Old Cause of the Jacobites, and thence with the theme of Scottish nationhood. The '45 was not a straightforward revolt of Scots against English. Most Scots opposed it; many English supported it. But Jacobitism, for obvious reasons, was bound up in the 18th century with nationalist feelings. It was a profoundly reactionary cause, and attracted support from the most backward parts of Scottish society; the feudal lairds who had failed to make their peace with modern commerce, and the near-barbaric clans.

Redgauntlet himself is a fanatic, almost a madman. For years he has devoted his great energy to fanning the dying embers of Jacobitism. It is a hopeless task. The clans, which provided the only effective troops for the Good Old Cause, have now been smashed for good. But Redgauntlet believes that his schemes are nearing fruition, and when good luck enables him to kidnap his long-lost nephew, Darsie, he sees this as further grounds for hope. The former feudal tenants and retainers of the Redgauntlet family will, he thinks, rise in support of Darsie, who is the true heir to the baronetage. (Darsie's father was executed for his part in the '45.) With this force, the Jacobites can capture Carlisle, and the many lingering supporters of the Cause will see that it lives again, and will flock to its standard. In anticipation of this happy event, Prince Charlie comes back to Britain disguised as a Catholic priest.

In the still-primitive country down by the Solway Firth,

Redgauntlet is a popular leader with real influence, and here he can still deceive himself with wild dreams. Even so, he recognises that it is the destiny of the Redgauntlets, according to old legend, to fight always on the losing side. He acts as he does, he indicates to Darsie, because he cannot help it:

> 'The privilege of free action belongs to no mortal—we are tied down by the fetters of duty—our mortal path is limited by the regulations of honour—our most indifferent actions are but meshes of the web of destiny by which we are all surrounded.' Ch. 8

His sense of destiny, it will be seen, is tied up with outdated feudal ideas. 'Honour', as he means it, is feudal honour—the vassal is honour-bound to serve his king. This view of destiny is partly true, but also very false. Whatever scope for free action philosophers may tell us that we have, it is clear that we act as we do because our heredity and environment have shaped us in a certain way, and this environment itself is shaped by history. Scott's insight here shows his true mastery. He makes the Redgauntlet destiny, a figment of the Middle Ages, symbolise the power of the past over our lives—and this is his greatest theme of all. But if history were really so straightforward as Redgauntlet believes, nothing would ever change, we would still be vassals and serfs. This, of course, is what Redgauntlet wants.

By making Darsie, a Redgauntlet himself, reject the destiny which his uncle offers him, Scott shows both by argument and example that such theories are false. The theme of the lost heir, which in *Guy Mannering* or *The Antiquary* emphasises the continuity of life, is here used to dramatise *discontinuity*. Darsie tells his sister that the Redgauntlet vassals will not rise, 'they cannot, at this time of day, think of subjecting their necks again to the feudal yoke, which was effectually broken by the Act of 1748, abolishing vassalage and hereditary jurisdiction'.

> 'Ay, but that my uncle considers as the act of a usurping government,' said Lilias.
>
> 'Like enough *he* may think so,' answered her brother, 'for he is a superior and loses his authority by the enactment. But the question

is what the vassals will think of it, who have gained their freedom from feudal slavery, and have now enjoyed that freedom for many years.' Ch. 18

The Redgauntlet destiny is broken with feudalism, though Redgauntlet himself is willing to carry it through to yet another bitter end. Out of generations of civil war, history has moved on to a new plane. We see the same discontinuity dramatised in *The Heart of Midlothian*, when Douce Davie at last relaxes his severe Covenanting principles and agrees that Reuben Butler should take a job under terms which they strictly forbid. History wears down the strong codes and causes which history itself creates.

Redgauntlet's conspirators assemble at last, in a wayside inn near Carlisle. They are an odd, timorous bunch—squires from Wales, Cornwall and the Border, the backward 'Celtic fringe'; and, of course, a Doctor from Oxford, the home of lost causes. Sir Richard Glendale, the most outstanding figure, bluntly describes them as 'the scattered remnants of a disheartened party'. Any hopes that they might really get down to their violent business are shattered when Redgauntlet has to admit that Prince Charlie has brought with him his mistress, whom they regard as a spy.

At this point, memories of Scott's other books crowd in; the dissolute Rothsay, the womanising James IV of *Marmion*, the conceited James VI, the lecherous Charles II—the faults of the Stewarts at every turn have assisted the inevitable downfall of the way of life which they represented. The theme of family destiny strikes up again when Sir Richard Glendale exclaims to the Pretender's face:

'My God, Sire! . . . Of what great and inexpiable crime can your Majesty's ancestors have been guilty that they have been punished by the infliction of judicial blindness on their whole generation!' Ch. 22

For here is Charles insisting, like Charles I before him, on his absolute right as a king to disregard his subject's wishes.

But once again, destiny is broken. When word comes that

General Campbell is on his way to confront the conspirators with the armed might of the Hanoverian state, the Jacobites prepare to die for their King as their fathers and brothers have done. Charles stops them; he is ready to meet the headsman's axe like his own ancestor; for a moment he rises to real dignity. But almost at once this courage is made to seem ridiculous. For the General arrives, like a schoolmaster, to warn the children that their game is over and they must all go quietly home. If they do this, there will be no arrests, no reprisals. Charles is now so lightly regarded as a threat by the Government that King George will be happy to see him sail away in peace. Suddenly Redgauntlet realises the falsehood of his own theory of destiny. All its feudal webs are broken, and he exclaims, 'the cause is lost forever'.

Once again—a brilliant touch this—a Campbell is made to represent the winning side: for the Campbells, through the generations of Civil War, had a gift for backing the winner. As Redgauntlet, alone of the conspirators, sails away with his Prince, disillusioned yet heroic in the manner in which he faces up to his new understanding of history, he takes the Scottish past with him—the wild clans, the brutal Border warriors, the passionate Covenanters and Jacobites, the nation itself. Yet he leaves Scotland exactly where it is; no longer a land of heroes, but a prospering region of the sort which King Louis XI would have liked to see and Coeur de Lion would have shuddered at. The citizens of Edinburgh are planning their New Town, the Carron ironworks is getting on its feet—and the American Revolution is about to usher in a new age of causes, and new violence, and new types of heroism. The theme of *Redgauntlet* is not purely Scottish; its subject is historical change, any time, anywhere.

We now see the function of those layers of introduction which we must peel off before we get to the meat of a Scott novel. Scott's introductions in his own name, written for the collected edition which appeared shortly before his death, set out his historical purpose. The fictitious 'editors'—Jedediah Cleishbotham, Captain Clutterbuck, Laurence Templeton, Crystal

Croftangry—are conceived as comic 'types' from Scott's own day. But their introductions, often very lively, are not there purely for entertainment. Their function is to relate the history of the novel to the Scotland of 1815–30.

In his introduction to *The Lady of the Lake*, Scott had explained how he felt able to depict the Highlands in a narrative poem:

> The feuds, and political dissensions, which, half a century earlier, would have rendered the richer and wealthier part of the kingdom (i.e., England) indisposed to countenance a poem, the scene of which was laid in the Highlands, were now sunk in the generous compassion which the English, more than any other nation, feel for the misfortunes of an honourable foe.

This illustrates a theme in Scott which is so all-pervading that we are in danger of missing it through its very obviousness—the theme of reconciliation and compromise. He believed—it was one of his Tory illusions—that the conditions of his day marked, or at any rate should mark, a final truce in society. He refused to see that a new type of social struggle was being born in the strikes and unions of the city workers. Because reconciliation between the middle and upper classes was nearing completion by his own day, he felt safe to praise and present sympathetically those who had opposed his own favourite causes, just as the English now felt safe enough to feel sorry for the clans. His 'signpost' figures—Morton, Baillie Jarvie, the Duke of Argyle—are often figures of compromise, who balance two warring sympathies. This was not untrue to British history. It is one of 'the peculiarities of the English', as a contemporary historian, E. P. Thompson, has called them, that the middle class never crushed or swept away the aristocracy, but came to terms with it—in 1688 and 1832. We see this peculiarity in the preservation of the monarchy and the House of Lords long after their original function has disappeared.

There is no compromise between Mary Queen of Scots and her enemies, between Burley and Claverhouse, between Ravenswood and Lady Ashton, between Rob Roy and the Law, between the clans and the modern world—Scott does not disguise the bitterness of civil strife. But he is always able to signpost the future with characters who see both points of view, or to foreshadow an eventual compromise by the sympathy which men feel for an 'honourable foe'.

AN ASSESSMENT

It may seem that we have written more about history, and even about sociology, than about literature. This is inevitable in Scott's case, and those who take a narrow view of literature will never care for him. Readers who prize delicate artistry more than they wish to extend their own knowledge of life will always prefer Jane Austen.

Scott, in our opinion, wrote two very great novels, *Waverley* and *Redgauntlet*. *Old Mortality* and *The Heart of Midlothian* touch higher levels than either, but false plotting lets them down. *The Bride of Lammermoor* is held back from greatness only by the relative weakness of Scott's 'romantic' characterisation. *Quentin Durward*, on a lower key than all these, is a masterpiece in its marriage of comedy and history. Other novels—*Rob Roy*, *Ivanhoe*, *Kenilworth*, *The Fortunes of Nigel*, *The Fair Maid of Perth*—are books which only a major author could have written, though they are seriously flawed. *Guy Mannering* and *The Antiquary* are basically light-hearted books, which it is easy to love, and their comic characterisation sets them with the best of Scott's work. And Dugald Dalgetty, who bestrides the *Legend of Montrose* like a coarse and talkative colossus, is perhaps the most delicious of all Scott's triumphs.

Even this does not exhaust Scott's good work (which is why we have dealt with the novels as a whole rather than concentrating on the best of them). His portraits of Mary Queen of Scots in *The Abbot* and of Cromwell in *Woodstock*; the quarrels in the Crusaders' camp in *The Talisman*; the evocation of landscape in *The Pirate*, are worth coming across, even in the midst of much poor writing. It is our own experience that Scott becomes an addiction, but it is to be hoped that critics will never reach the point, long since passed with Shakespeare and Dickens, where his worst writing becomes a subject for acclamation. Scott was a snobbish, prudish, reactionary, and in some ways very vain, man, who wrote far too much and pressed on even when he knew that a novel would be bad. He is also one of the most rewarding writers in our language, and one of the great figures of world literature.

Bibliography

1 SCOTT'S WORKS

The list which follows is not complete; it omits his miscellaneous prose works, among which, however, his *Life of Napoleon Buonaparte* (1827) should be remembered, if only because it took him such pains to write.

Poems and Plays

There is a collected volume (first printed in 1904) in the Oxford Standard Authors series. Individual works of note are:

The Chase, and William and Helen (from the German of Bürger), 1796
The Eve of St. John, 1800
The Minstrelsy of the Scottish Border, 1802–3
The Lay of the Last Minstrel, 1805
Marmion, 1808
The Lady of the Lake, 1810
Rokeby, 1813
The Bridal of Triermain, 1813
The Lord of the Isles, 1815
Halidon Hill (a dramatic sketch), 1822
The Doom of Devoirgoil (melodrama), 1830
Auchindrane, or, The Ayrshire Tragedy, 1830

Novels

There are numerous collected editions of the novels, of which the Everyman Library contains one of the best. Individual titles are:

Waverley, 1814
Guy Mannering, 1815
The Antiquary, 1816
Tales of My Landlord (first series, *The Black Dwarf* and *Old Mortality*), 1816
Tales of My Landlord (second series, *The Heart of Midlothian*), 1818
Rob Roy, 1818
Tales of My Landlord (third series, *The Bride of Lammermoor* and *A Legend of Montrose*), 1819
Ivanhoe, 1820
The Monastery, 1820
The Abbot, 1820
Kenilworth, 1821
The Pirate, 1822
The Fortunes of Nigel, 1822
Peveril of the Peak, 1822
Quentin Durward, 1823
St. Ronan's Well, 1824
Redgauntlet, 1824
Tales of the Crusaders (*The Betrothed* and *The Talisman*), 1825
Woodstock, 1826
Chronicles of the Canongate (first series, *The Highland Widow*, *The Two Drovers* and *The Surgeon's Daughter*), 1827
Chronicles of the Canongate (second series, *The Fair Maid of Perth*), 1828
Anne of Geierstein, 1829
Tales of My Landlord (fourth series, *Count Robert of Paris* and *Castle Dangerous*), 1832

In addition we have Scott's:

Journal (1825–1832), edited by J. G. Tait and W. M. Parker, 1950

and his

Letters, edited by H. J. C. Grierson and others, 12 volumes, 1932–1937

2 OTHER BOOKS

The standard biography of Scott is still the one written by his son-in-law, J. G. Lockhart—finely written, but heavy going in places. Lockhart's *Memoirs of the Life of Sir Walter Scott* was first published in its fullest version in 1839. The Everyman edition is a reprint of Lockhart's own abridgement. John Buchan's *Sir Walter Scott* (Cassell, 1932) is a lively and perceptive brief biography. There will soon be a new life by Edgar Johnson, whose life of Dickens is the standard work.

Two recent histories of Scotland are J. D. Mackie's short *History of Scotland* (Penguin, 1964) and G. S. Pryde's *Scotland from 1603 to the Present Day* (Nelson, 1964). Henry Hamilton's *Economic History of Scotland in the Eighteenth Century* (Oxford U.P., 1963) fills out many important details. David Daiches's *The Paradox of Scottish Culture* (Oxford U.P., 1964) is an excellent short introduction to the 'mind of Scotland' in the 18th century. E. J. Hobsbawm's *The Age of Revolution* (Weidenfeld and Nicolson, 1962) gives a panoramic survey of Europe in Scott's lifetime, and provides a social context for Romanticism.

In *Scott and Scotland* (Routledge, 1936), Edwin Muir makes a brief but provocative attempt to explain Scott's position in Scottish culture. David Craig's *Scottish Literature and the Scottish People, 1660–1830* (Chatto and Windus, 1961) deals with the historical and cultural questions which Muir raises at greater length, and still more provocatively. His remarks on Scott are perverse, but well worth reading.

The best way of getting to know the Edinburgh society of Scott's day is to read Lord Cockburn's *Memorials of His Times, 1779–1830* (A. and C. Black, 1856). No complete edition has been published for sixty years, but the book is well worth the trouble it may take to get hold of it. In a delightfully dry and witty style, Cockburn relates many anecdotes of Scott himself and of the judges, advocates, professors and preachers of the period. A. J. Youngson's *The Making of Classical Edinburgh* (Edinburgh U.P., 1966) tells the fascinating and significant story of the growth of the New Town.

There is a serious shortage of good criticism of Scott, and many of the novels have been sadly neglected. There is a learned and helpful paperback by Thomas Crawford, *Scott* (Oliver and Boyd, 1965), in the Writers and Critics series. Two very difficult, but very rewarding books are Georg Lukacz's *The Historical Novel* (Merlin, 1962) and Alexander Welsh's *The Hero of the Waverley Novels* (Yale U.P., 1963). Lukacz's monumental study gives many pages to Scott; while he sees Scott as a great popular writer, Welsh's book reminds us that his Toryism had a cutting edge to it. An American book which has not yet been published over here is Francis R. Hart's *Scott's Novels* (1966), which does deal with every novel, and makes many worthwhile points.

Otherwise, one must scavenge for scattered essays. William Hazlitt's in *The Spirit of the Age* (1825, now in Everyman) is still stimulating reading. John Ruskin's chapter in the fourth part of his *Modern Painters* (1856, now in Everyman) still has more to tell us about Scott's poetry than most recent criticism. The most telling modern contribution, Donald Davie's short lecture on 'The Poetry of Sir Walter Scott', is so far available only in *Proceedings of the British Academy*, XLVII (1961), where it is worth seeking out. Karl Kroeber, in *Romantic Narrative Art* (Wisconsin U.P., 1960) makes some useful points about the structure of the narrative poems, and some sensible ones about the novels.

Donald Davie has also published good essays on individual novels, in his *Heyday of Sir Walter Scott* (Routledge, 1961), but most of the book deals with other writers. Other valuable points are made in Arnold Kettle's *Introduction to The English Novel* (Grey Arrow PB, 1962), and David Daiches's *Literary Essays* (Oliver and Boyd PB, 1967). Finally, Ian Jack has a short pamphlet, *Sir Walter Scott* (1958) in the Writers and Their Work series (Longmans), and a long essay in his *English Literature, 1815–1832* (Oxford U.P., 1963).

General Index

Index to Scott's Works

Deans, David, 18, 19, 128, 133, 141, 146